11 / 5

DITCHED by DR. RIGHT

DITCHED by DR. RIGHT

And Other Distress Signals from the Edge of Polite Society

Elizabeth Warner

· · ·

VILLARD ⟨V⟩ NEW YORK

The names of the characters and aspects of the events described
in this book have been changed, so as to mask the identities of
the paramours, friends, family, and colorful acquaintances
who got me a book deal in the first place.

A Villard Books Trade Paperback Original

Published in the United States by Villard Books, an imprint of
The Random House Publishing Group, a division of
Random House, Inc., New York.

VILLARD and "V" CIRCLED Design are registered trademarks of
Random House, Inc.

ISBN 0-8129-7392-5

Printed in the United States of America

www.villard.com

2 4 6 8 9 7 5 3 1

Text design by Simon M. Sullivan

This book is for Dr. and Mrs. Silas Llewellyn Warner,
who spawned many of these stories and all of their teller

CONTENTS

• • •

DITCHED by DR. RIGHT

carbon dating

* * *

This is a true story.

When you grow up in the Protestant blood clot that is suburban Philadelphia, there's very much *a plan* at work. One is typically weaned, whelped, and privately schooled, whereupon you move on to the roost-and-spawn phase, with the occasional rinse & repeat. And that's that. The plan is proven, it's time-honored, it's genetically appropriate. Curiously, however, it neither applied to nor worked for me.

In my case, the best-laid plans of mice and men are best left to mice and men.

As the youngest of seven (the next child being seven years older), I grew up in a family that remains astonished I can button a garment and walk upright at the same time. Nor will this change. Were I to develop a fun, easy, at-home way to split the atom, or stem the tide of Parkinson's disease, they'd still say, *Oh, the little one? She doesn't do too much. But she has nice hair.*

They're pretty sure I put the *I* in *inertia*.

My mother, a pathologically elegant woman whom we'll call the Widow Warner, has maybe four big concerns. The Four Horsemen of her Anglican Apocalypse are

1. post-Soviet Communist domination;
2. my marital status;
3. osteoporosis; and
4. the network cancellation of *JAG*.

On the day I announced that I was considering a departure from Manhattan, in order to try a Year Abroad in Los Angeles, nobody really knew what to do. Although everyone certainly had something to say. (The Year Abroad actually turned into several, but that's another story.)

Plus, my proposed relocation seemed even more implausible given that until recently I had regarded Southern California as a kind of backyard to the Antichrist. It was New York's slower, spoiled, thicker, and more slothful sibling (and I'd never even seen Canada).

Mother was shocked. Then worried. Then horrified. And finally, what-on-earth-am-I-going-to-tell-people *bewildered*. For one thing, she has always viewed California as a kind of lost, vestigial Spanish colony. And two, she's long felt that human interaction, fiscal negotiating, and air travel are not the kinds of things her youngest should try to tackle unsupervised. I reminded my family that they had all seen my initial move to New York—where one's entire net worth would no doubt be forcibly removed either at gunpoint or at Barney's—as yet another testament to my immaturity.

Apparently nobody could recall ever saying anything of the sort. I was sure this and other observations had naturally been relegated to that emotional cedar closet that every youngest child has, which is always chockablock full of accusations, observations, pronouncements, and edicts elder siblings will eternally deny ever having made.

Additionally, we all well remembered that our own greataunt (a noted ambassador, playwright, and significant backer of causes that seemed uncomfortably Aryan to me) had always said, "California? You can't get a Goddamned thing fixed in Southern California when you want to. And when do they always tell you it'll be ready? *Mañana. Mañana.* Everything's *mañana.*" My siblings and I had ignored what may have been her senility, her cultural imperialism, or her genuine racism.

Of course, the Year Abroad *idea* would simmer codependently for a long while. In the time it might take to (*a*) groom and promote a boy band, (*b*) triple the U.S. national debt, or (*c*) run out the lease on a Jetta, I would acquire some small degree of penny-wisdom. I would fall hopelessly in love with a bright, grumpy, whinging journalist. With whom I was smitten, and who was funny, like you read about. We would be charitably referred to as the Jew and the Shrew. I would spend my twenties stumbling haplessly through the greatest city on earth. I would become wildly proficient at a job that was as heady and rewarding as it was toxic. I would disappoint and embarrass most of my family. All this before I could summon the capacity to awkwardly stare doubt, familial roadblocks, and nonrefundable airfares in the face. And even begin to consider boarding the last Leap of Faith train to the coast.

Nor would any of this have transpired had it not been for the swiftly agonizing departure of one Dr. Right. Here's what happened.

Everything began one Ides-riddled March. When I had the world by the tail. Or at least by a hind leg. I was a Senior Promotional Copywriter at Time Inc.'s Consumer Marketing Group. This is the in-house advertising agency responsible for the promotion of some twelve magazines to the general public. I authored persuasive marketing copy to readers and consumers. The goal was to bring in new magazine subscribers and keep them on board for the rest of their lives. I was most definitely part of the plan. And thus far, it was working. I was going to live snappily ever after. I had a superb office with several windows and an enormous hexagonal coffee table, largely because I could. I authored million-dollar sweepstakes. My job was to lure unsuspecting Middle Americans into purchasing magazines they didn't want, wouldn't like, and probably couldn't read, all with the promise that they'd love the sneaker phone we'd also send them the instant we got their check or money order. With really tangible results. If we did our job well enough, which I almost accidentally did, we could whip Middle Americans into such a buying frenzy that they'd eat their young if they thought there was an AM/FM clock radio in the deal.

I was genuinely enjoying a kind of secular rot in New

York City. But in a good way. The kind of spiritual decay that's actually quite comforting, particularly when it's complained about in smart, buzzy bistros brought to you by the colors *taupe* and *veldt*. I had a one-bedroom apartment slightly larger than a votive candle in an antiseptic but deceptively cheery part of midtown Manhattan. And most essentially, I was enrolled in a rigorous program of healthy, expensive psychotherapy.

It was a lovely, mindless time of income and ascent. I couldn't help but bask in the burl walnut finish of familial approval. My family—especially my mother—was delighted. *The little one's on her way. She's a three-bedroom co-op away from the rest of her life.* The best part? I was living with, sleeping with, scheduled to build a future with (and quite satisfied by) a good-natured anesthesiologist heretofore known as Dr. Right. Who really was my soul mate, my future, and the love of my lifestyle. Together we frequented parties where the women all wore black suits and that shell-shaped jewelry that's supposed to look modest but was purchased with proceeds from IPOs of little start-ups like GM and Exxon. And the impossibly appealing men with that ruddy, Northeastern skin that wants to shout "sun" and "tropics" but really whispers "gin."

Which may be why, on that lovely spring morning as I watched Dr. Right leave me, I began to spiral and suddenly found myself formally introduced to the concept of introspection. He'd skulked out the door on Gucci-clad cloven hooves, into the stunning, dappled daylight of disgrace and taxis. And he'd dropped his bags dramatically at his feet, and he'd looked up at me and wiped his brow in that noonday-sun kind of way that men do in deodorant ads and Steinbeck novels. Leaning out our third-floor window, I had said, "Don't forget this"—and catapulted his prize brass cigarette lighter out, watching as it bounced expensively on the hood of his beloved convertible. And he had looked back up at me, a meaty Teutonic fist clenched in defiance, and said four parting words.

Four words.

"Don't scratch the enamel!"

To anybody observing him glancing helplessly up at me with his Poppin' Fresh Dough eyes, his would appear a desperate and soulful plea for one last try, for some kind of reconciliation. It actually wasn't. And I knew better. I'd seen that fawn thing before. And no way was I going to jump right back into Lake Him. Still, I was the one physically, palpably, and incomprehensibly racked with guilt. Absolutely riddled by it. And that would be *why?* Why? Why had I spent two years with a man who was so blatantly unable to see the earth's passage of time as anything other than one long autumn afternoon in Connecticut? *And we lived in New York.*

Don't get me wrong: this was a terribly attractive guy. Clark R. M. Wheeler, M.D., wasn't a brain trust, but he *was* one of those people with an uncanny sense for what was *relevant.* He had sort of a cultural suntan. The kind of guy who'd invoke an arcane but incredibly hip name reference—and invoke it *disparagingly*—at parties. But enough so that people would figure, if he could disparage, then at least he could comprehend far better than they. He'd say things like *"That woman there thinks she's Susan Sontag."* Or he'd deliberately mix up Jean-Paul Belmondo and Jean Paul Gaultier so people would think film *and* fashion. *How multimedia.* Or he'd remind us all at brunch what a profound impact, *ya know,* the Velvet Underground had had. Dear Nico. And how the mood on Prince Street just hadn't been the same *since Andy died.* Of course, privately to me he'd inquire about things like whether Lanford Wilson and August Wilson *were* actually brothers. Or just cousins. And I remember one evening at a big dinner party hearing him refer to Tony Blair as a *technocrat.*

I'd pulled him aside and said, "Don't you Yvette Mimieux *me,* Clark. Do you even know what a technocrat is?"

"Not at all," he'd answered, "but nobody *here* does either, so I'm fine."

I had genuinely loved him. It was that good, comfortable, this-is-how-it's-going-to-be love. Born of time, afternoons, and I'm here, you're here, let's-make-dinner ease.

And I could say not one word when he left. Not a single one.

Given the world of Marketing & Promotion, which claimed me as an early, willing, postgraduate casualty, I'm not without the blemish of *veneer* myself. After all, I do write promotional materials for a living. And have always been a little stunned that people paid me (and financed my health and dental repair) just to sit around and dream up ideas to coerce unwitting or distracted people to make purchases, buy magazines, contribute to political causes, and join any number of clubs. I am amply rewarded for creating a huge and growing expanse of wilderness between Americans and their income.

Copywriting is not rocket science, but it does have its own experiential learning curve. I created contests. I dared Americans not to believe that they *might have already won.* I kept dreams alive because I authored million-dollar sweepstakes. And renewals. And bills. And *you-like-this-magazine-why-not-try-this-one?* pieces of direct mail. And everything comes Risk-Free, and it all has a Free Gift of marginal value attached somewhere. And the fact is, I had a certain knack for it. It was as if God had said, *That fellow? I'll make him lead a country out of war.* Or, *That child? He'll bring hope to Zimbabwe.* And then He'd said, *That one? The little redhead? She'll be aces in the junk-mail arena.*

Junk mail is one of civilization's great gifts. It's a necessary evil for a number of reasons. One, it allows people to live reasonably comfortably in antiseptic midtown-Manhattan co-ops. Two, it saves companies millions, because when they only want to reach, say, five or six million people but they don't want to reach an additional eleven million people (who'd never buy their product anyway), they simply send out direct mail. It's perfect. A genuinely targeted way to spend only what they need, to wind up in exactly the right mailboxes.

At lunch with literate, moral types I say I'm in publishing. At cocktail parties, I just go ahead and admit I'm in advertising. And thus, when I met and fell for Clark R. M.

Wheeler, M.D., I have to say I kind of knew what I was getting into. I had a pretty good rent-stabilized Glass House myself.

Plus, things with Clark had been coming along kind of swimmingly. We'd met at an auction (my first and last, his 546th) to benefit either Russian dissidents or glaucoma or Kurdish unity, and we had both gotten terribly drunk. Clark lit my cigarette but announced rather boldly that he didn't want me to think he was one of those guys who went around lighting people's cigarettes. Not that I cared. He smiled a lot after he said things, as if startled by his own ability to speak, and then he'd look at you like you'd shared some inside joke about his newfound skill. Which I thought was a *huge* connection for us.

After about three weeks of rather formal courtship, Clark and I entered into an emotional lease agreement. After another three months we were perceived as dull and sweatered.

Until sixteen months later, when he announced that he could no longer deny the woman who had touched his soul. And it turned out, she and I were not the same woman. In fact, she was my very own cousin, a feral, oppressively blond homemaker with a penchant for Joyce Carol Oates, olestra, and Kansas—the *band*.

And with that, Clark said, he wanted to explore other avenues. Just breezily, like people say they want to reduce their carb intake. And despite the fact that I hoped they'd be avenues teeming with late, machete-wielding bike messengers, I said nothing. I simply affixed both eyes upon him (easier said than done, since I have a bad wandering eye—the left one is frequently at a ninety-degree angle to my nose). I just glared. Silently. Before shedding one tiny, Lifetime Cable–ready tear. Whereupon I began to clean. And then he was gone.

Twenty-eight minutes later I called my psychotherapist, an Andie MacDowell/Nurse Ratched hybrid. I left a whining message on her machine, and she left me one two hours later, saying she'd love to see me, but the Jitney to Quogue was boarding in three minutes—and maybe I should go back home to Philadelphia for a stint, "because you always feel better when you do." And then she said also not to forget to love myself a little, and also not to forget that I still owed her for January.

So, convinced that this woman might just have a point, and equally convinced that my entire body had atrophied from too much peanut butter directly out of the jar, I decided to get some exercise. So I went for a drive. In a taxi. To Penn Station. And I boarded Amtrak's *Yankee Clipper* to Philadelphia. To my mother's home. Where she, a forthright woman in her seventies—who very definitely still likes Ike—would assure me that this was fleeting. And that somehow all would be well. There would likely be a bubbly tub involved. And I would be offered Shake 'n Bake and other cholesterol-infused Gentile Home Remedy products.

Once back inside suburban Philadelphia's Main Line, I knew I would be subjected to the gentle ridicule, wishful thinking, and abject criticism that doubles for parental love in so many of these families. I think.

"Mom," I whined as I walked inside. It smelled of cedar and wet dogs. "Mommm, he left me."

"Who? That wooden Indian?" She hugged me and I was suddenly, tearily petite.

"Claaarrk. He . . . he—"

"Sweet thing," she cooed, squeezing me for a long time. "There," she said. "Not to worry, Lovebug. You know you're much better off without that Clark. Reading all that Philip Roth nonsense. Hmm. Is your hair lighter? What's with those little tendrils?"

"He just up and . . . he didn't even . . . I mean, *nothing*," I wailed, again hurling myself like an unwanted medicine ball into her lanky, aproned torso. "This is awful. An affair? That's the last thing he'd . . . what'm I going to . . . *I don't know what to do!*"

"I do."

"What? *What*, Mom? What can you *possibly*—"

"We'll get supper. And you're going to feel much better, Miss Pink." She patted me and strolled over to get a better glimpse of the kitchen's thirteen-inch TV set.

I continued to blurt interrogatives and demi-expletives, but she'd stopped listening. See, *Entertainment Tonight* was profiling the leisure activities of pop superstars. Which prompted her to turn back to me and observe:

"And another thing, Lambchop. Say what you will, but that Céline Dion's got the most beautiful golf swing I think I've *ever* seen."

I was home. That which Anglo-Saxons call "healing" had begun.

Mother told me to put on lipstick and then we'd be off to dinner. I silently followed her around like a wan Labrador while she turned off lights, shut doors, and made little notes for herself on monogrammed Post-its. She is tall and slim, with pale blue eyes and hair that is quite gray, but I don't so much see the gray, because in my mind it is auburn. She talks with her hands. She drives cars passionately, swiftly, and efficiently. We sped along Lancaster Avenue, and I recounted a few details of Clark's departure as I followed the telephone wires in the darkness outside the car window. Finally we pulled into the Merion Cricket Club's massive red-brick entrance and wound along past the acres of lawn-tennis courts, parking in a huge lot filled with Jeeps and small expensive sports sedans bought to replace now-matriculated children. Once inside the clubhouse bar we ran smack into Thatcher Longstreth, our family lawyer for over two centuries. Mom gently held the back of my neck like one would an unwieldy but valuable trophy statuette.

"Hiya, kid," said Mr. Longstreth, slapping me hard on the back and permanently lodging an olive in my trachea. "How's that job? And the big city? Still saying no? And how's the wandering eye?"

"Oh, hi. Everything's fine, thanks." I was now really listless.

"The littlest is back to pay us a visit from the Big Apple!" My mother beamed, and I was relieved by her bland remark. This is a woman who might just as easily have said, *She's back to lick her wounds . . . the needless foolish we-told-you-so wounds inflicted by that poseur jackass from Wesleyan with two heads and the stupid haircut and dubious medical degree.* The nice Irish lady who had been smiling at me since I was four years old appeared and ushered us into the main dining room for supper. Mom waved good-bye to Mr. Longstreth and steered her Littlest Cub ahead. I kept my head down as we entered, still curious about whether or not the diagonal diagrams on the carpet would ever make me dizzy enough to throw up. They hadn't thus far, but they were looking like they could.

I behold our club's cavernous Sistine-esque dining room, and suddenly I am fourteen again. Mom has taken my big sister Meg and my two brothers Malcolm and Eliot here to lunch. Meg is complaining that someone made fun of our family earlier that morning. And surveying the brood proudly, Mother says, "Well, I have four very competent, very attractive children."

There is a pause, whereupon Meg turns to Mother and says, "You know, I don't think Elizabeth's such a knockout."

My uncle says later that the Lord has given everybody something, and that it's a good thing He made Meg so astonishingly beautiful because He also gave her the mind of a tropical fish.

Mother now surveyed the dining room, and I wondered when, if ever, I would be able to look around pleasantly like she does, and not think about dying quietly and alone, curled in a walk-in closet, with the tips of dry-cleaning bags tickling my nose. We were seated, and I picked at radishes and celery lingering in easily two inches of water in a porcelain dish. I remembered that most people who drown do so in less than three feet of water. But I don't remember if that's because they're in the tub or because sharks like shallow shoals.

"Lambchop, I know it feels terrible, but you really are better off without him. You just *are.* I can tell you right now that if your father were alive, he wouldn't have cared for Clark one bit." Mom smiled at the waitress, who was waiting patiently. "Just the little filet. Rare, Margie. Thanks."

"And no veggies tonight, Mrs. Warner?" Margie waited quietly with her pad.

"Certainly not. What about you, Lambchop?" Mom and Margie stared at me.

"Well, um, how's the monkfish?" I queried.

"Elizabeth, it's fish. It's *fine.*" My mother was exasperated, as if I'd asked Margie to recite Farsi.

So I wouldn't cry anymore, I quickly changed the subject and told Mother about how I might be accompanying a friend to the Tony Awards.

"Oh, that'll be fun. Has Pete Gurney got a Tony nomination this year?" she asked hopefully. Mention theater and she'll always carp about how A. R. Gurney never gets the recognition he deserves. Now that Dick Rogers has passed on. (Although she does concede that Dick Rogers got plenty of recognition.) Gurney is a really big deal for Mother.

"I don't think there's a Gurney play up for a Tony this year, Mother," I admitted, with the same gravitas I would use to tell her that somebody's nation was too racked by poverty and civil war to send a troupe of athletes to the Olympics.

After a gin-soaked but nostalgic meal, with three side trips to the ladies' room, where I sobbed off and reap-

plied the makeup Clark R. M. Wheeler, M.D., had single-
handedly sent streaming down my already raw cheeks,
Mother and I returned home. In through the mudroom,
which was neither muddy nor roomy. With the cedar and
the wet-dog smell and the down vests nobody wears. The
house whose internal topography I know so well—all the
kids do—that we could each maneuver anywhere through
the dark barefoot, with only floor surfaces and the echoes
of certain walls and clocks and faulty ice-makers to guide
us. Mother suggested we retire to the den for a belt and a
visit.

The den reminds me of one thing and one thing only:
nature programs. *National Geographic. Wild Kingdom.* Jacques
Cousteau. And that Public Television programming mitz-
vah, *Nova.* I think these shows embodied a certain American
ideology that my parents were happy to imbue us with. For
one thing, they represented triumph from the get-go, beginning as they always did with powerful and heavily orchestrated theme music that invariably reeked of victory over
adversity. Then there was the voice-over, taking us through
the seasons. The gentle tone, ever assuring us that despite
the ravages of winter, all will thaw and spring will come.
And when spring—naturally characterized by the feminine
pronoun—does appear, her accompanying image on the
screen was usually time-lapsed footage of a flower opening,
with water trickling soothingly in the background. Then, to
further describe the newness of spring, came a shot of four
or five clumsy but alarmingly cute cubs—of canine or feline
variety—roughhousing, with the gentle reminder that soon

enough any one of these frisky little fellas would be large enough to systematically annihilate a small family of unwitting tourists, if provoked and hungry. Leaving nary a blood-soaked ligament.

But what always stood out for me with these shows was a kind of *morality*. Or its agonizing absence. Because about two thirds of the way through each program, a young wildebeest would get brutally mauled by a group of roving (and presumably delinquent) hyenas. Or a pair of cheetahs would take out an enfeebled gazelle. And I would watch this carnage in mute horror. And the question that always sprang to my lips was *why*.

"Why? WHY? Mother!?" I had demanded as a child. *"Why doesn't the cameraman step in and save that baby/older doomed animal if they can film it? Why? Why?"*

And Mother would always put down her needlepoint and look at me before saying,

"Because that's *nature's way*, Lambchop. That's nature's way."

And I just know that privately she had to be wondering the same thing. And that her response to me was just some kind of antidote to the existential void. And then she'd invariably look at the big wall clock behind me and say:

"Okay, Miss Pink. Isn't it time for Betty White's Party?"

Betty White's Party was our family expression for bedtime. An expression that, I realized some eleven years later on a particularly disastrous date, was *not* a universally recognized term.

As I retired upstairs that night, Mother pointed out that

tomorrow would yield banner opportunities to move on or at least to forget. Soon I wouldn't even remember any old Clark R. M. Jerk anyway.

"You know, Lambchop, that thing was never meant to be. You've got to let him go. You know what they say about a caged bird singing? When you let him go and he'll come back if he was meant to, but he can't know till he sings and flies, right?"

"I think I know what you mean." Then she told me that I should just get busy at the office, where there appeared to be less doom. Of that she was certain.

"You've got to keep the accent on the right *syl-LA-ble*, dearie. Why don't you just throw yourself into your work? You know, where you don't ever have to worry about forming close personal relationships?" She smiled, adding, "Oh, and here you go. I couldn't resist."

She presented me with a wrapped Lanz nightie. Which made fifteen this decade alone. A great woolly gown to keep the chilliest, burliest lumberjack toasty and impervious to nuclear winter for several unpleasant centuries.

"Thanks, Ma. You're right." I kissed her.

"God bless," she said as I ankled up the stairs.

I considered Mom's work-immersion advice. I remembered that my boss's boss had recently remarked that I'd have been considered quite attractive during the Middle Ages. And that it was just a good thing I had hair, what with my features and all.

Nor was I really certain that my mother understood exactly what it was that I did for a living. In the same way that men she knows who were in the war who did *anything* connected to planes are automatically "fighter pilots" (with whom she will discuss *Thirty Seconds Over Tokyo* until sunrise). This is exactly why I wasn't sure she knew what it was I did. And while I do not believe she thinks I am a fighter pilot, she has never once focused on the fact that the endless sweepstakes and renewal notices she gets in the mail were probably authored by her youngest child. I'm pretty sure Mother thought that since I worked for a magazine empire, and since I wrote for a living, I must actually have been a journalist.

Of course she was right about the getting-busy part. Wisest to get back on the plan. So I would become subsumed by my job, forget all about Dr. Right, and feel that sense of serene calm that comes from good old head-in-the-sand hard work. I would be, after all, functioning. And I would find the answer. And it would be direct mail.

I then crawled into one of the mirthless barracks-style twin beds in "my room." It was, in fact, still my room, even though it too had undergone that whitewashing process that people perform to create a generic guest room when the kids have gone. I know this causes problems for many people. People who feel forgotten and alienated once the space they grew up in (and slept in, wept in, journaled in, played 45s in, and viewed dirty pictures in) has been utterly transformed. Transformed until their beloved sacred spot is no more personal than a "demo sleeping chamber" at Calico Corner. Still, I can take comfort in the fact that mine are actually parents who *would* have kept trophies displayed even now, if I had ever won any. Looking around, I had to smile, because even though the plaster Christmas hand imprints were gone, I could distinctly make out a small stack of *Ranger Rick*s on the bookshelf—although *My Friend Flicka* and *Black Beauty* had long since been delivered unto grandchildren, replaced now by volumes from Winston Churchill, William Buckley, and Amy Tan.

I noticed a shiny new catalogue on the bedside table. (Editorially speaking, a well-crafted catalogue really can reside comfortably and alone on the summit of direct mail's Mount Olympus.) I hadn't authored this particular one, but it was clearly a handsome example of this important genre. What's not to like about catalogues like these: four-color shiny invitations to a Better Way that will require some fiscal outlay on your part? I am all too happy to invent the bright, customer-friendly worlds of bold colors, attractive copy blocks, and undeniably appealing lives and styles.

On the catalogue cover, in an upbeat, devil-may-care font: THIS SUMMER. So summer's upon you. So there's that. You're reminded, ever so gently, that you're quite likely to be stuck in lederhosen and a hair shirt this summer unless you buy some clothes. And damnit, you'll need that one cotton sweater, color: *surf,* that's good for exactly one afternoon when, by golly, you better be sitting Native American—style on a dock talking animatedly about this week's issue of *The New Yorker* because—jiminy!—you actually got through it and it only took you seven hours.

Then you open the catalogue up. And behold. Extraordinarily attractive people, seemingly devoid of concern.

The kind of young, scrubbed people who, if you asked them about domestic abuse or Kabul or stem-cell research, would probably produce one of those red plastic rings on a stick from a reinforced on-seam khaki pocket and *blow a soapy bubble right through it at you.* Those khakis that are, of course, available in *shale, slate, silt,* or *schist.* And next spring in *pesto* and *alloy* and *root* and *hemoglobin* and *lentil* and *inlet.*

Suddenly you wonder why *you* don't have a boyfriend who wears eight layers of plaid shirts all at once. And why doesn't he bring you the fresh milk that he's just happily procured from the goat . . . the goat grazing delightfully by your handcrafted knotty-pine and wrought-iron trellis? Why doesn't he bring that milk to you as you're reclining languorously atop that downy, sunlight-flecked bed that is covered by a bold, colorful quilt? The quilt *you* stitched last summer while you laughed happily at your Adirondack fishing hideaway with your good, straight, white, appealingly liberal friends before joining forces to make a healthy but robust meal together filled with laughter, humility, and pointed intellectual debate. And even when you had a flat tire it was fun, because those guys you're with—the ones with all the plaid shirts—see, along with the fact that they all have doctoral degrees in Semiotics and a profound understanding of Mahler and can explain the difference between wicker and rattan, why, they're also uniquely qualified to change a tire in less than ten minutes, plus they can operate a forklift, and they'd also ably run with bulls in Pamplona.

Which is when I closed the catalogue, took three Benadryl sinus tablets, and enjoyed a hot mug of Sambuca. Before I drifted uneasily but antihistaminically into raglan-sleeved, garment-dyed sleep, a cursory check of my answering machine in New York revealed that Dr. Right had indeed phoned, but simply to let me know that he was returning to retrieve his nine iron and his "Paul Stuart Elements of Style" CD-ROM. And he'd phoned, he said, *so as not to startle me*. But now, of course, nothing startled me, and as I considered the gyrations and machinations of the human spirit, I came to realize that it was all, really, just nature's way. Just nature's way. Besides, I was eating. And frequently in top-flight restaurants. And it dawned on me that perhaps one *can* coexist peacefully with—or at least graze alongside—one's black heart and empty life.

The following morning I returned to New York with renewed vigor. Sometimes you just need a little trip home to see that once we overcome the Gaza Strip of childhood, anything's surmountable. Even Susan Sontag.

is the medium the message?

* * *

Mother had said to me, as she had to each of my six older siblings, that if upon graduation from college we chose to live at home, we would be absolutely required to pay rent. And even though I couldn't imagine why anyone with functioning neurological impulses and prehensile grip would even *consider* living in the gutless mix of adultery and tonic that doubles for suburban Philadelphia, I still thought Mother's stance pretty draconian. It was, however, certainly effective, and when we left school each one of her brood immediately jettisoned him- or herself to a major urban center, seeking a new view, a better life, or drugs (and in the case of two siblings, all three). I'd been a lousy student, and having surgically extracted a bachelor's degree from an upstate college, Mother had said that perhaps I'd fare better in the working world. My dad, on the other hand, had stressed the importance of morality and ethical behavior and of giving something back . . . but nobody ever listened to him. Besides, everyone in Philadelphia felt that if you weren't somebody in corporate America, you were nobody on earth.

Plus there was a prevailing sentiment that it was about time that I, who had never succeeded at much of anything, might learn to do something successful—or at least profitable—for a change.

Six months after graduation I was ensconced in an antiseptic neighborhood, with the copywriting job at the huge media megaconglomerate, and for about twelve minutes Ayn Rand suddenly made a lot of sense. One couldn't help but feel inspired walking daily across town to Rockefeller Center. It was the commute to which all other commutes aspire. And despite a childhood marked by unbridled failure and not a few physical shortcomings, I did have an alarming knack for promotion.

And thus, rather than wait for someone to let me manage their orphaned-wildlife refuge in Kenya, I'd gone to work at a company whose culture I adored. Whose marketing prowess was unequaled. And whose cafeteria and attendant Fixin's Bar spawned a wistful envy from everyone laboring in the lesser media megaconglomerates that lined Sixth Avenue.

Even when I went back to Philadelphia, my decision was always reaffirmed, because at parties, having developed military-intelligence-level overhearing skills, I happily picked up audible phrases of contentment from my mother, phrases like "our youngest" and "settled in New York" and "Time Inc." and "steady paycheck" and "401(k)" and "success" . . . and I could sleep easily. Or at least stop listening in.

Finally, after all those years I'd spent as a worthless buck-toothed crosseyed nobody, my prelarval overactive imagination had become a chrysalis of efficiency. I was needed. I was useful. With a place in the world. I clung to the bizarre notion that millions of Americans counted on me daily to direct their purchasing decisions. This was life-affirming stuff. I would live—and thrive—through direct mail. I would harness every single creative bone in my body, and with a startling vehemence I would pour my energies into writing copy.

I suppose at first I only felt the twinges of morality intermittently, like a charley horse. And, despite being totally unaware of the slow hemorrhaging of my soul, I was, after all, eating out a lot. And of course I was also in a rigorous program of psychotherapy. Every Wednesday at 11:30 A.M. I walked the twenty-five blocks to my psychotherapist's office. Genteel, whip-smart Eleanor Cogan, Ph.D., had been keeping me steady and even for the better part of a decade. Hers is one of those quintessential Park Avenue doctor's offices, cocooned in privacy and utter anonymity. It is on the ground floor of a superb gray limestone co-op, with the kind of old-school doormen who know exactly how to gauge your emergence process from a taxi, who know when to open the car door, and when to reach inside to help with packages.

Dr. Cogan's office is a spectacular tribute to taste and

unobtrusiveness. Every week I would stare at the curtains in the waiting room, at the mahogany of the secretary's desk, at the silk striped couches, and wonder if anyone could feel that this was unattractive design. It is *that* universally appealing. Completely smooth, quiet, and unshowy. Just nice. Even the watercolors on the walls are of violets. Who can argue with violets?

Plus, Dr. Cogan represented to me everything I was not. She worked with inner-city schoolchildren. She devoted her time ceaselessly to literacy programs. She counseled pregnant teens for free. I always knew that she was what I would have become if I had been a good person.

At this point I really was winning my own personal Focus War; I was compelled, driven, and humorlessly efficient. Naturally, business was humming along. In fact, as a result of my efforts, Time Inc. had attracted a bit of unintended attention. I'd written a piece of wildly successful direct mail that lots of people didn't throw out. A direct mail solicitation for one of our most successful magazines—a piece of white paper with a yellow carbon-paper backer that said simply "Please Pay This Amount," followed by a dotted line that led to "82 Dollars for a Year's Subscription." Unwitting consumers had believed it to be a bill for a subscription they'd already ordered. So they paid us at once. In full. For a full year of the magazine. The checks had come pouring in, until such time as my direct mail piece was brought to the attention of the kind of folks whose job description requires them to frown on this sort of thing. I had assumed that everyone would naturally be delighted to have quadrupled business. Half of my siblings, the more liberal-minded ones, had been horrified when I recounted the details of this imbroglio. I received a letter from one brother, a tax attorney who drove a pickup truck and listened to Bruce Springsteen a lot, in which he said he didn't know me anymore, since I'd been *soaked in the starter fluid that was greed, and that maybe when I emerged from the Black & Decker vise grip of corporate America, we'd have something in common.* I wrote him back and reminded him that he was, after all and in the end, *still an attorney,* so he might as well just step down off that cross before he tore something.

Right before my soul evaporated entirely I began to have terrible nightmares about direct mail, about being assaulted with million-dollar sweepstakes checks the size of surfboards and of living on a desert island where there was no food, water, or emotional sustenance—just a daily airlift of direct mail. However, I did not believe for a second that the dreams were in response to some kind of moral higher ground I was subliminally scrambling toward. Plus, I was still arrogant enough to regard people who thought about stuff like that as poseurs, who belonged right up there with poets, jazz, and Warhol aficionados.

I started to look at the other patients who came and went from Dr. Cogan's office. None of them appeared particularly highbrow or arrogant; none of them served as the Devil's Letter Carrier, as I did. In fact most of them embodied a kind of friendly worry, or a troubled middle-management malaise that made me feel even more guilty as I contemplated the silly things I discussed with her. Things that had very little to do with important matters of life, death, and sustenance in the real world, I thought. I began to sleep three nights out of every five.

I now viewed the entire world as an evolving marketplace, and soon even my language was peppered with slugs, headlines, and catchphrases. It started almost imperceptibly at first. I'd remark to a friend that her *relaxed-shoulder garment-dyed jersey was really a great fall look, echoing that nineties demand for simplicity and comfort.* Doing the place settings at Christmas dinner, I would ask Mom whether she wanted me to put *the crisp linen napkins out or opt for the soft, velvety cotton ones reminiscent of cherished meals of bygone days. And which* color *napkins, Ma,* I'd ask— *ocean, marrow, or pine?* Then I'd ask her if I should set them all out together in a delightful holiday array that would bring cheer to the whole family.

I couldn't stop myself. When we'd decide upon a restaurant for the evening I would say things like *Great, so let's act now, there's not a moment to waste!* One day my friend and I entered a discount luggage shop and I involuntarily blurted out to the clerk that we were *seeking storage solutions that would make any weekend getaway a snap!* I announced to my ninety-five-year-old great-aunt that she'd be happier if she *started thinking outside the box and let the digital revolution wash over her.* Another time I warned a horrified salesman at Barney's that I wanted *real value and unparalleled craftsmanship for my hard-earned dollars.* The fact that I was buying socks was really beside the point.

Then one night I'd come home to my apartment absolutely exhausted. But it was that old-fashioned Arthur Miller kind of exhausted. Where of course you're susceptible to just about anything on TV because you know if it's in an ad, you can buy it, because *by golly you've earned it* . . . and if it'll help clear a sinus passage or soothe lower-back *anything*, you know you want it because *you are* the market. *You* are the modern American victim of Modern America. Whose rampant, infected consumerism you'd helped create. And that's when with slow horror I finally realized what I had become. That my transformation into a twisted, mediapathic Nazi was all but complete.

The phone rang, and I was reminded very curtly by my prep-school roommate that in twenty-four minutes I was expected at cocktails on East Seventy-fourth Street, at the home of a new couple she believed had hung the moon. *So,* she'd said to me, *I don't want you drinking and doing all that arrogant liberal soliloquizing—particularly since we all know what you really do for a living. Don't you dare mention socialism or your newfangled lefty notions and how your blood sugar depletes when you have to go above Fifty-ninth Street. And for God's sake don't wear one of those skirts you got at Strawberry, okay?*

I hung up the phone and found the soberest, most acceptable clothing I could find. I located an appropriately snotty silk scarf and knotted it in a way that I hoped would indicate that I was really extremely carefree and successful, despite the fact that I was edging toward a horrible morality crisis, and that I believed I was little more than a scavenging, well-heeled monster.

Thirty minutes later I was ushered into the elevator of one of those fancy buildings where the doorman actually gets on with you, as if he believes you are likely to pilfer some of the elevator's chrome molding if left alone. I entered an apartment that finally made me understand the word *appointed,* while a murmuring and slightly frightening man in a cutaway removed my coat and directed me into a cavernous living room filled with attractive, shiny, purposeful, non-guilt-ridden people. Everything in the living room was beige, with couches that could comfortably accommodate entire UN delegations and probably had. The paintings were tastefully lit from below, the kind of paintings that never have signatures—and then you realize you've also seen them replicated on notecards in museum gift shops. I was immediately accosted by a self-appointed court-jester figure who obviously thought John Hughes movies could be viewed as ironic learning tools. I extracted myself gently in that way you do from people who are behaving strangely but who might have had too much to drink and could therefore detonate, causing a vitriolic, crystal-breaking embarrassment.

The women all wore smart diagonal-print wrap dresses or bright silk blouses atop dark wool crepe trousers. The men all had one hand in their pocket and rocked back and forth on expensive Italian (or Belgian) slip-ons that had obviously never, ever, touched more than three blocks of pavement. Many of them cupped short, wide tumblers of scotch or bourbon or rye, inside of which ice cubes bathed and raced to melt before being swallowed. Every single person here knew from (and could spell) *aubussons.* The music was tastefully Latin in that way chosen by young adults who live only yards west of Madison Avenue, who have finally rejected Bobby Short but who still recognize the need for subtlety (and something that works sonically with clinking glasses).

Some of the women nibbled on watercress, and I furtively witnessed one of them actually ingesting an entire jumbo Gulf shrimp when no one was looking. My old roommate rushed up to me and, after appraising my dull attire, explained that our host and hostess were over there, talking to another young couple I knew. When people asked what I did for a living and I told them, they'd smile knowingly at me and say, *"Oh, that's smart."* I was introduced to our host, a magnetic tall man with that kind of lazy, nautical ease that is so uniquely American. He extended his hand to me, then smiled and presented his wife, who, to my horror, was also my psychotherapist. I stammered an introduction and she winked at me, in that way of psychiatric protocol with which I was all too familiar (since my father—also a shrink—had frequently been put in the awkward position of socializing with patients in our hometown). She made no mention of our preexisting relationship and was exceedingly gracious; and after an hour of general mingling and flaky, creamy, creepy, braised, skewered finger foods, my roommate again raced up to me and asked if these weren't just the most fabulous people I'd ever met in my born days—and wasn't it such fun for a stick-in-the-mud like me to be meeting new people in the first place? And it was all so diverse, she said, what with lawyers *and* bond traders!

At which point I said my good-byes and slithered downtown to another gathering, where I believed I would be welcomed with open and decidedly nonsuccessful arms at a friend's loft on Thompson Street.

As I approached the apartment I was struck by the notion that I was no more likely to find amenable people there, no matter how earnest, lovely, arty, and unfettered they might be. It occurred to me that I could go on this way until I had a bleeding ulcer and a Saab.

And so, with that small realization, I quickly turned on my own cowardly cloven hoof and returned home to bang out a letter of resignation and try to get a good night's sleep.

the wandering (private) eye

. . .

When I was younger I thought it would be fun to write a
novel, in that way that ignorant, foolhardy types with bachelor's degrees who can operate a stick shift think it would be
fun to open a restaurant or prep for a pentathlon. Still dripping in the amniotic fluid of career promise and unable
to rent a car legally, I always thought I'd author something
that would be called "scathing" or "wickedly irreverent" or
"oddly infectious," but soon realized that probably wasn't
going to happen. The hitch here being that implicit in *writing* a novel is the assumption that one isn't entirely averse to
reading one. And for me, reading a real book . . . we're right
back there with the restaurant and the pentathlon. But of
course you can't tell people that. So I'd hold my head up at
brunch and say, *Me? I prefer the magazines.* The periodicals. The
catalogues. And with any old offense being the best defense
these days, I'd boldly ask who needed traditional literary
stimulation when you got the Ring Cycle every single day in
your very own mailbox? It's true. *Vanity Fair,* nine months

out of twelve, isn't a magazine. It's a meal. The bottom line was, of course, that people who read books intimidate me. At parties I still find myself struggling to keep up when someone talks about being consumed by the latest tome on schizophrenia, or somebody else is happily lost in a poignant saga of three generations of powerful women. I'm not actually sure when—or if—I really ever *came of age,* and for that reason the notion of reading about someone else doing it makes me pretty uncomfortable, no matter how triumphant that snowy peak is when the protagonist finally gets there. For several years I genuinely marveled at John Irving's powers of self-congratulation (not that I'd read him) calling that book *The Cider House RULES!*

But here's the what. When I do read, which is pretty much when I forget to pay the cable bill, I only like one kind of book. Espionage. A good, heady, bomb-strewn but breathless romance set in war-torn Europe. And I have learned that when you're at a dinner and genuinely interesting people are chattering about whether *The Corrections* should have been in Oprah's Book Club, no one—no one— wants to hear about wiretapping and explosives used in 1943. Recently I found myself immersed in a novel about the literally billions of dollars' worth of art stolen from Jews by Nazis during the war and then hidden—to this day—by the very collaborationist Swiss. And I came to a paragraph where our hero, an Israeli assassin—but a good guy—finds himself trapped in an elevator with an attractive Russian cellist. And it said, "He could feel her nearness, as he smelled her French tobacco and good soap." At which point

I wondered if *I* would ever be trapped in a crawl-space environment like this. And if ever a man would behold me that way. Whether he'd appreciate my Neutrogena Dry Skin Formula, or whether he would wrinkle his nose at my decidedly not French Marlboro Ultra Light smell, before wondering just how much dog hair there was on my sweater. As I read along, it occurred to me that perhaps I'd never really wanted to write a novel in the first place. And that the reason I read just these kinds of books was simply because all I really wanted was to be a spy. Which immediately brought to mind the first time I'd ever had the whiff of intrigue. Here is what I remember about that:

When my previously divorced parents married each other, a big *second* wedding was absolutely not the thing to do. Because in 1961, if you'd blown it the first time and had kids to boot, it was wholly inappropriate to celebrate that second chance publicly, in front of either the Lord or Philadelphia society. Each of them brought three children to their marriage, and I was born a year later. Which does, actually, make me Tiger.

Mom's first husband had no trouble with her new family; he is lovely, and he and his third wife spend Christmas with us to this day. My father's ex-wife, however, was perhaps not so wild about his new marital situation. His children were delivered on weekends by a Pleistocene nanny with explicit instructions about their care and feeding. I think she was probably always on the lookout, always eager to uncover an evil—or at least negligent—pattern of behavior on his part. But the two sets of kids continued to spend weekends getting to know one another, and in this way we somehow formed a family.

Autumn, with its crisp nostalgic austerity, was always our favorite time of year, largely because of football. My father, a die-hard Princeton man and seemingly unable to get over that fact, thought it essential that we kids were raised in the gridiron tradition. Thus on Saturday mornings we all drove to Princeton, or Cambridge, or New Haven, or Hanover, or wherever drunken, starchy, disassociated Ivy League fun was to be had. Mostly, though, we liked the home games, and so for the first fourteen years of my life every other fall weekend was spent at Palmer Stadium in Princeton, New Jersey. This being the early seventies, there was not nearly so much to do on the New Jersey and Pennsylvania Turnpikes en route home. There was no Vince Lombardi Rest Area, no Molly Pitcher Convenience Stop with McDonald's. The Meadowlands still enjoyed a modicum of tranquility and class as a wildlife preserve and biohazard refuge.

This being the case, my parents' greatest dilemma became finding a spot where they could each have a cocktail and that would also be somehow fun and appropriate for the brood. And, naturally, a place that would prove suitable in the report to my father's first wife. We spent months looking for the perfect family spot. And when we did finally find the Lucky Dog Grille & Motel, also billed as "the Tristate Area's premier & preeminent lounge and cuisine spot," we knew our odyssey was over. As we approached, a sign outside read

WHETHER IT'S BOOZE OR A SNOOZE YOU'RE BEGGING FOR, JUST COME "SIT" AND "STAY" AT THE LUCKY DOG!

And that we did. On each visit, Dr. Warner's brood was greeted emphatically at the Lucky Dog Welcome Desk by a dapper little man who, in addition to being a sort of a Lucky Charms prototype, could perform any number of card tricks that stunned us all. The Lucky Dog was a true haven. Every Saturday night Armand, the maître d', rushed out from the dining room to meet us, spewing kisses and unintelligibly foreign phrases. Then he would shoo us along to "Dr. Warner's Top Dog Table." He'd also often declared that Dr. Warner's Top Dog Family was "without compromise," which none of us understood.

The dining room itself was cavernous, with a burgundy shag rug, velvet banquettes shaped like bundt cakes, and salmon walls done in that bas-relief-style wallpaper from which designs protruded like bumps on a topographical map. The wallpaper depicted (in 3-D) deliriously happy, chubby women from the late Renaissance period, frolicking and swinging gaily behind tiny pimplike satyrs lurking nearby. We could never resist running our fingers (regardless of what fruit or candy extract happened to encase them) over the wallpaper bumps. Until my mother realized that part of what we were rubbing was the women's protruding breasts. Which was when she suggested we refrain from this kind of touching, *tout de suite.*

The tablecloths were pumpkin-colored, made of a very dense linenlike fiber that withstood the repeated test stabbings we gave it. Essentially, it was a bit like eating dinner inside a very cozy bedroom slipper, or maybe in some serial killer's van.

The waitstaff was nameless, faceless, and charming. We were really the only regular guests besides those that stayed in the Lucky Dog's adjoining motel. The routine was always the same. My mother ordered bourbon, my father vodka, while seven Cokes automatically appeared at Dr. Warner's Top Dog Table. There were those requisite radishes and celery in little white dishes. The kids always ordered the same thing—seven hamburgers, always preceded in my case by one incongruous order of escargot. My own meal was never complete without these bonus snails, which I devoured because I thought they somehow illuminated my adultness. I was about six, and summarily ignored. With orders complete, we were excused and free to roam the Lucky Dog, which included a stop at the Welcome Desk to bother the Lucky Charms Clerk, whereupon we'd proceed, as a pack, to the motel behind the restaurant, where vending machines and a neat ice maker beckoned. In fact, the entire meal was always punctuated by requests for quarters for these repeated trips to the vending machines, where we'd usually encounter any number of motel regulars, who were always extremely friendly, if a little weary.

For some four years, we all thoroughly enjoyed our Saturday night visits to the Lucky Dog Grille & Motel. Not even my father's ever-vigilant former wife, always on the lookout for some kind of negligence on his part, could object to our beloved family tradition.

Until one evening when we all disembarked from the Country Squire wagon, typically excited about dinner at "the Dog," as we'd taken to calling it. After ordering, we kids beelined it to the vending machines, embroiled in our long-standing debate about the ingrediential vs. aesthetic difference between a Clark bar and a Butterfinger. As we turned the corner by the ice machine we saw six or seven huge men standing and staring at the machines. When they noticed us they turned and glared, and one nodded at us. Two of my brothers stuck out their hands and offered the men a shake, announcing that we were Dr. Warner's Lucky Dog Top Dog Family. The big men stared at one another, and one of them spat on the floor. I had never seen anyone spit indoors. Then the biggest of them smiled a little and said, "Kids, what say you get your Hershey bars and beat it, okay?" Which is exactly what we did. We raced back to the table and breathlessly told the story of the huge men who had banished us from the vending machines at the back of the motel. My mother listened and explained, sensibly, that the men probably wanted candy very badly and that sometimes people become irritable when they're hungry. The big kids accepted this explanation, but living almost exclusively on a diet of *Adam 12* and *The Untouchables,* I was certain something was amiss.

After eating our salads, we returned to the vending machines, where, to our shock, there were now six or seven different huge men plus four ladies who greeted us warmly. I remember that the men's hands were each about the size of a healthy rabbit; their knuckles were red like they'd banged into things a lot. There was no way that even two of these men could have fit together in the front seat of our car. Three of the ladies had tennis shorts on, but instead of sneakers, they wore shiny high heels like tap dancers might. The fourth lady, who wore a long fur coat banded with horizontal leather stripes with the same tap dancers' shoes, immediately smiled and asked us our names. We were delighted by the attention and lingered with the ladies for another ten minutes, until one of the men looked over and asked if maybe our parents were looking for us . . . and shouldn't we be getting back to dinner? We left, only to return after dessert, mesmerized by the crowd now congregating next to the vending machines. Only this time there were three brand-new women. As before, the women beamed and gave us each a little wave. Several of them had very bright lipstick on, and they each had rows of white teeth, like brand-new kitchen tiles. One of the ladies asked us to do cartwheels; another one patted my head and asked if I'd like to try some of her perfume, a heavy, musky rose scent in whose pungency I delighted for the next three days.

We'd been chattering away with the friendly ladies for maybe fifteen minutes when I heard loud voices over by the ice machine. We could discern one of the women saying, "They're not hurting anyone," and another lady stepped up on her behalf, saying, "They're just kids . . . who gives a damn?" At that moment two of the men started to shout at her, and I heard words like "Effing no good little effing kids" and "They're gonna screw everything up!" before my sister took me by the hand. Suddenly other men joined in, and next thing we knew, it was absolute chaos. Everyone began to shout about "those Goddamn kids." Then one man, the burliest of the group, actually slapped a lady across the face, causing her to yelp, and then he did it again. Which made her scream. A scream that could be heard, we were sure, across several parking lots. My sister clamped down hard on my ears and pulled me very close to her side; by this time all of the men were cursing and the ladies were shrieking and I heard one man shout, "Get those freaking teenyboppers outta here, Lorraine, they're gonna ruin this whole Goddamn thing . . ." and before I knew it there were other voices and suddenly Armand and the Lucky Charms Clerk came running to our aid and then I heard someone yell "Police!" and like a shot we all ran down the corridor to the restaurant, where my parents, oblivious to it all, waited quietly with seven parkas.

As we pulled out of the parking lot I marveled at the police cars that were now streaming into the lot. "Wonder what that's all about," I heard my mother say, and then I fell asleep in the way way back of the station wagon.

The following morning the phone rang at seven-thirty, which was not unusual, as Dad had patients calling at all hours of the day and night. What *was* unusual was that it was one of our neighbors, calling about the Lucky Dog. Mother answered the phone, looked quite stricken, and said to my father, "Barbie Norris says your first wife's not going to be thrilled about that place we've been taking the kids to after the games." And sure enough, within minutes one of the local papers was delivered; a headline screamed: "Football

Team's Dirty Little Secret Uncovered; Mayhem Prompted by Tiny Sleuths." Pictured was the big spitting man, who was, as it turned out, a well-known football player. Next to him was the woman who had sprayed perfume all over me. Whose name turned out to be Miss Basilica LaFemme. And who was now referred to as Madame Ringleader. Three enormous Pennsylvania state troopers were also pictured, beaming judiciously next to two more of the big men we'd seen the night before. The article went on to describe how the commotion raised by several unidentified children had called attention to a major call-girl and racketeering operation that both the Philadelphia Police Department and the Pennsylvania Brotherhood of State Troopers had been attempting to infiltrate for two years.

We never returned to the Lucky Dog Grille & Motel. But by then, HoJo's had a Fish Fry and a complete cocktail menu and we ate fried clams regularly and forgot all about our whistle-blowing days.

noncolonial williamsburg

● ● ●

My best friend, Kate, had called and invited me to a party
in Williamsburg. Nor did she mean the silver-bracelet-
making, olde-blacksmith-observing, book-bindery-visiting,
stockade-touring hamlet in Virginia. Rather Kate meant
the once-desolate, then white-hot, now just coolly essential
part of Brooklyn. And she had phrased the offer in that way
that friends do who need a copilot at arrival. Someone who
will have the presence of mind to make her own way over to
the bar and chatter with people nonsensically of her own
volition. To this end, I knew my role on that Friday evening
was basically to perform the time-honored Best Friend
Duty of being little more than a clean, reasonably educated,
and vaguely witty warm body. I would be, in the big scheme
of things, viewed as furniture with basic neural response.
Someone who could be counted on not to yell or throw up
or accidentally shatter crystal and laugh awkwardly. She'd
also pitched the invitation by saying that it was actually a
birthday party, which I regard as the tried-and-true Party

Softener. Birthday parties seem somehow *nonthreatening*; you know that for at least 30 percent of the time you and the other strays will confide to one another that none of you actually know the person being feted—or even which one it is. As it turned out, I knew both host and hostess, although I still haven't any idea whether the birthday belonged to either of them.

When Kate gave me the details I'd also recoiled at the thought of a gathering in an area that I didn't particularly like. I'd always found this part of Brooklyn almost aggressively tedious. As NoLita had been, and TriBeCa before it, this was the kind of place that tried really, really hard to make you think that it was uniquely different from other neighborhoods, since it was ostensibly devoted to some kind of late-nineties art-as-commerce manifesto.

Williamsburg apparently had a *purpose*. It was an enclave that *didn't have to advertise*. Similarly, I found the pretentiously unpretentious use of lower-case Courier fonts on addresses and storefront signs sort of creepy. And the habit of calling bars "boites" and the ubiquity of terms like "atelier" and "lounge" seemed equally off-putting to me. I made mental notes of the names of places and marveled at restaurateurs' ability to find something cool in naming spots randomly. I had always wondered when New York bars with names like Wax and Boom and Spy might inevitably give way to cooler, chicer spots with names like Window or Brakepad or Grapefruit or Harangue. Williamsburg was also a place where people whom I normally respected claimed that lofts whose price tag could finance most of America's aerospace exploration were somehow still considered "finds."

"Plus, of course, there will be lotsa cute boys there," Kate had added. But she'd said it only to bolster her argument. As people do who need yet another selling point to toss into the atmosphere, regardless of authenticity. With the same degree of care and actual knowledge as if she had declared that there would be beach balls or self-stick envelopes there.

Then she told me what else would be there. And There It Was. The Real Reason behind her invitation.

An opportunity to meet up with a guy with whom she was entirely smitten. A man I knew only vaguely, and whom I found a little slippery. Jeremy Somebody. Of course he'd been quite attentive, phoning Kate regularly, and in person he had an appealing, if studied, manner. He was also smart and lethally handsome, in spite of his then-popular Roman centurion haircut. Still, I found him dubious at best, for reasons I couldn't quite pinpoint. But I'd also learned long ago not to offer up commentary and criticism where love—or at least artistic and sexual synergies—were at hand, so I kept my mouth shut and went, spending the requisite federal grant needed to taxi from midtown Manhattan to Williamsburg.

The loft was smirking and spectacular. It belonged to Marcus and Cecilia. Marcus was a young, up-and-coming sculptor of marginal talent and stunning looks, who had announced *sotto voce* during our greeting that his personal mission was to create awareness of the constantly realigning global economic marketplace through papier-mâché. It was rumored that the size of their loft was also duly proportionate to a windfall his father had incurred in a highly speculative offshore banking operation. I had no idea what offshore banking was, and as I swallowed the first of many nonpitted olives whole, I could only envision an ATM bobbing in the waves next to a windsurfing instruction pier at Club Med. I smiled and asked if, given the sheer spatial volume of his apartment, Marcus was also trading precious metals and foreign currencies on the side? I suspect my remark was neither funny, welcome, nor correctly timed.

Workwise, Cecilia was a self-described "devotee of the written word" and claimed to love Williamsburg, although you also knew she was the kind of girl who, if she needed so much as a pack of Chiclets, would be hundreds of blocks north at Fairway in two shakes of a lamb's tail.

"It's so great down in this part of Brooklyn," Cecilia confided to me in the bathroom where we'd gone together to chat because girls can. "There's so much space for me to . . . to . . . to read in, and all."

"Space is good," I said, trying to sound pensive and actually emulating Yoda.

"And the light here's *so* good for Marcus's work," she said.

Personally I felt Marcus's murky anthracite-and-battleship-gray pieces could benefit from considerably less illumination, but I kept that to myself.

Soon enough we spied Kate's quarry. Jeremy was a young filmmaker, I had been told. We were introduced, and he smiled one of those deliberately amused smiles that men give, during the three seconds of which he had assessed my sexual capabilities, my net worth, my contact potential, and probably my dog's weight. I knew he was also actively forgetting my name. Between phrases Jeremy touched his chin in a thoughtful way, and while this gave him a certain air of introspection, I preferred to suspect it was a kind of involuntary mourning for what must have been a failed goatee. He explained that he made ends meet doing production work, which totally impressed Kate. I could see the little wheels spinning in her head as she envisioned her lothario making cool and calculated decisions on a sober documentary film set, working long hours while he watched dailies and thought about moral imperatives. I decided never to point out to her that our fair Romeo was, in truth, likely to be wandering around lost in subzero weather in appalling black Reeboks with the requisite fanny pack and self-important headset arrogantly yelling, "Copy that!" and asking for people's "twenties" into a large and cumbersome walkie-talkie before herding stray film extras toward some frenzied Craft Services lunch line. And as I actively avoided three actresses who would no doubt tell me about their *Law & Order* stints, I paid close attention to what Jeremy was saying, listening carefully so that in approximately five weeks when Kate was bobbing haplessly like some forgotten buoy in the harbor of shocked despair, I could be reasonably comforting.

People had gathered at the bar, actually a midcentury stainless steel desk that hemorrhaged cool. The kind of desk I knew some poor Jack Lemmon–style insurance adjuster had once toiled behind for forty dollars a week next to thousands of faceless others, before the desk was Given a New and Affluent Life by ABC Carpet & Home. The conversation turned to current political crises, serving simply to create a polite social duck blind from which everyone could survey the room. By this point Kate had managed to lean her head upon Jeremy at least four times. I focused my attention and tried to be cheery and interested. Jeremy had a practiced pallor and knew exactly when to appear shy, self-effacing, or both. He was explaining to her the basic framework of a novel he was working on.

Realizing that Kate had already plummeted into an obsessive abyss, I tried to look on the bright side, which I was sure I would locate at some point. Jeremy, it turned out, had been born and raised in New York City, something, he explained, that made him truly unique. He told me that upon graduation from Sarah Lawrence he had followed the aura of Joseph Heller back to NYC into a four-hundred-foot garret on East Fifth Street. Kate beamed in wonderment. When the conversation turned to movies, he confessed that he didn't actually like Scorsese or Tarantino but preferred those Merchant-Ivory "weepies." A bell went off in my head because this seemed to me the kind of thing guys like him wanted girls like us to think. And also because I had heard him speaking rather exuberantly about *Reservoir Dogs* and the *pure balletic rush of Peckinpah* seconds earlier to someone else.

"I genuinely admire you, Jeremy," Kate said. "Yeah. It's really . . . it's so *inspired*, what you're doing. It must be extremely labor-intensive to write a book." I sidled up to catch some of the teeny hearts that were popping out of her eye sockets like lovelorn lemmings. I wondered how he would respond, and thought it would be hard to assess, since I knew nothing of literature and considered myself entirely devoid of book appreciation, understanding, or knowledge.

"I've always loved words," he told her. "I mean, who doesn't? They're the ultimate form of expression." Obvious, but okay, Jeremy.

"Plus, I'm used to rejection," he explained, "never welcome but inevitable. But like they say in France, you sort of *have* to be in this business." Okay. So far so good. Still no Code Red. Although I'm not aware of the French saying anything about rejection. But when Jeremy announced to Kate that *the media was the carcinogen of the masses,* tiny alarms ricocheted throughout my skull like cars at a Berlin intersection. Then he touched Kate's arm and said that he'd be happy to furnish her with some good books. I thought this a nice gesture and started to think that I might be just an overcritical jerk, until I heard him offer to start her off with some Joan Didion or Anaïs Nin—or even Michael Musto— *'cause they were really good. Because, Kate, they're all about the process and the product.*

When he suggested that she allow him to take her to dinner the following week at a nice little bistro, I saw that I was little more than your garden-variety bitter, paranoid best friend nursing a broken heart. After all, he hadn't said a nasty thing about anyone. He hadn't been cruel or used *option* as a verb. So I decided to shut up.

"I mean, who am I to say this," he said, "but, you know, books are important. They're . . . they're, actually, they are really the antidote to *wonder*. I have to ask myself questions daily, or I lose air."

He turned to me and said: "Don't *you* wonder all the time?"

I had tried to shrug but just twitched a bit, because the things I wonder about, like why Fresca is opaque or why the Betamax failed, are not the kinds of things genuinely interesting people wonder about. Finally I wandered off in search of friends and managed to amuse myself for a few hours. I tried not to think about my supremely unattractive streak of mistrust and the fact that I always managed to conjure up the worst in people.

Around midnight I strolled into what I thought was the master bedroom in search of my cigarettes and wound up in an anteroom filled with six or seven of Marcus's many creations. I stared at the great huge papier-mâché globes and the angry red finger paint smeared on them to indicate, I guess, the impending doom that would surely befall all of us, if this artist was right. On a large yellow legal pad that sat atop a blond-wood desk someone had written the words "Annihilation—Castro mind Fuck?" and "SINN FEIN" in angry block capitals, while underneath, in a decidedly feminine hand, was the message "M—please pick up paper towels, Snackwells and litter for Puff—XOXO."

Next to me the door into the bedroom was ajar, and coats lay on the bed. I spied Jeremy fumbling around at the bureau as he put on his coat. I slowly entered and he smiled warmly, his lips curling upward in proportion to my approach. On the bureau behind him I noticed many bottles and vials of tinctures and skin-care products. The result, I could only imagine, of a Kiehl's airlift.

"Aren't they astonishing?" Jeremy asked me, picking up a bottle of some decidedly floral-smelling unguent. "Have you ever seen so much *product*?" He marveled at the labels. "I'm absolutely overwhelmed by all this . . . this . . . this—"

"Wonder?" I volunteered, and he laughed. A gracious laugh because I was a jerk.

He ran his fingers slowly along the labels.

"And how about that papier-mâché?" he said.

"Yeah, " I said, suddenly feeling really stupid about art.

"You know," he said, "you probably know just as much about art as anyone else here. Don't hide your light under a bushel."

He winked at me and explained that he wasn't actually leaving but was going out to the fire escape; in a whisper he added that *he tried not to smoke in public.* I returned to the party, kicking myself for thinking such unkind thoughts about people who were simply more confident, thoughtful, and accomplished than I. Why had I been so quick to judge—so unmoving in my view—when quite possibly I was simply bummed because a cute boy liked one of my best friends, and resentful because they'd probably be conjoined carnally later?

At about 2 A.M. I asked Kate if it wasn't yet time for Betty White's Party, she being embroiled in a frantic word game on the floor involving tiny sheets of paper. *Absolutely not.* She was going nowhere. Then she squeezed me.

"But thanks for coming down here with me, Doll. You rule!" I knew I didn't rule. I sucked. So I left.

The following morning I phoned our hosts to thank them for the party, only to find Cecilia weeping uncontrollably. She explained, between sobs, that five of Marcus's papiermâché globes had been stolen and a keyboard had been destroyed by a wayward glass of Goldschlager. And if that wasn't enough, she sobbed, *all of her skin-care products had disappeared.* Like thousands of deep-cleansing, hydrating, aerating, and de-emulsifying dollars' worth of stuff. This last heist seemed particularly curious to me, but I kept my mouth shut and offered my help, before calling Kate. Unfortunately, she'd become so drunk that she was unable to account for her or anyone else's whereabouts the evening prior. I asked whether Jeremy had left before or after she'd lost ocular capacity. Ummm . . . she wasn't really sure. She guessed he'd just drifted out, but nobody was certain when, where, or how.

"But you know," she reminded me, "mmmm . . . he's flawless. And we *are* having dinner next week."

Jeremy was never seen or heard from again. By anybody. Ever. Kate remained stunned by his attention and subsequent disappearance. People talked about that promising young novelist who had seemingly fallen off the face of the earth, but everybody reasoned that writers tend to disappear. I agreed, although I couldn't name one off the top of my head who actually had. Kate would soon be swept up by the affections of a playwright whose specialty included the modern French farce, and before long Jeremy, the Kiehl's cat burglar, was all but forgotten.

life at the pet shop

• • •

During the time it took the United States to conduct the Watergate hearings, to witness the abduction of Patricia Hearst, to backpedal brutally out of war, and to watch as Al Pacino, Jon Voight, and Rosey Grier became household names, I was banned from my brother's bedroom.

Malcolm, the second-youngest and seven years my senior, had lobbied for this restriction, and my parents, in a surprise decision, had upheld his request. The fact that they backed him was absolutely shocking. The sanctions had been imposed as a consequence of my careless investigation (and destruction) of all his model airplanes—from Apollo lunar modules to aircraft carriers and U2 spy planes to B-52 bombers. All because of one bored afternoon when I had inadvertently decimated his entire fleet. What my parents didn't know was that he'd also been so furious at the time that he'd brutally held me down, placed cocktail olives in each of my nostrils, made me swallow nine crumpled pages of Mad Libs, and affixed some three hundred decals bearing the NASA logo to every exposed portion of my squirming, helpless body.

But as I said, it was a simpler time. The suburbs weren't a metaphor for anything. There was no Ikea. Calls had to wait. There was no cable. There was no irony.

With the five big kids away at boarding school and college, Malcolm and I waged a lengthy Cold War with an uneasy Swiss neutrality granted our parents and the many animals who shared our house. Animals were taken quite seriously in the home. In fact I assumed that all households had four dogs, a cat, three iguanas, and twelve finches (each bird named for a particular saint because that was when my sister was flirting with a subsequently aborted conversion to Catholicism). The earth's many creatures were frequently the topic of impassioned discourse at the dinner table. Christmas holidays always included exhaustive birding expeditions in Florida's Everglades, each trip imbued with that typical Northeastern Protestant gravitas.

We did, however, all glean a healthy ornithological knowledge, and more than once have I taken pride in my ability to distinguish catbirds from starlings, anhingas from cormorants, and wood ibises from the stunning pink roseate spoonbill.

And as far as the family was concerned, anyone who hunted recreationally was a Philistine. Period.

My father's psychiatric patients came to our house daily, where they were invariably accosted by any number of dogs and cats, whether they liked it or not.

Animals served as a metaphor for life. They lived, we

were taught, as *we* should, respecting their own projects, not nosing into everyone else's affairs. And putting on their plates only that which they knew they could eat.

Which is why on the day Malcolm gleefully left for boarding school, giving us neither a backward glance nor any explanation about what we were supposed to do with his eight-foot boa constrictor, things got a little complicated. We had no notion about its care. Let alone how on earth we were supposed to feed it. As my mother and I put Malcolm aboard the train to Boston at Philadelphia's 30th Street Station, I remember his words:

"Just feed him a mouse every two weeks—unless of course you can find a rat. Then he's okay for a month. See you at Christmas."

I had looked up at my mother, a resolute but elegant woman in her forties, and I know now that the only thing then that she hated more than George McGovern, margarine, and that subversive upstart Stephen Sondheim were puzzling, slightly creepy situations like this one.

At the dinner table the topic of where to purchase a mouse for Malcolm's snake to eat came up. My father excused himself instantly, as he was interested neither in snakes nor in the procurement of their prey. Of course all I could think of was the fact that a certain embargo had been lifted, and that I was now all alone in the house, free to roam my brother's bedroom, pillaging at will, playing LPs with abandon, and happily singing along with Buffalo Springfield and every single band that had ever played anything live at Budokan. And I was far more interested in mastering the words to "Guinnevere" and "Winchester Cathedral" than in absorbing subliminal life lessons about mice and death.

The following morning Mother announced to my father that the two of us were going to find a mouse if we had to visit every pet shop on the Main Line. Twelve minutes later we were in Bryn Mawr, significant to me because it boasted the only pharmacy where one could find Bonne Bell Lip Smackers, Wacky Packs, and the entire Jean Naté bath canon all in one place. Mother took me by the hand, and we marched into Dawson's Pet Store, a venerable institution that had provided pet supplies to Philadelphia families for centuries. Mr. Dawson, the owner, was the kind of man who always seemed startled when you entered his store, as if he had been touching something dirty. And, despite what was clearly an enormously profitable business, he always had egg yolk or toothpaste on his tie, and his shirttail frequently protruded from his fly. He always wore short-sleeved shirts of a color that would now be described in catalogues as *bran, dune,* or *early wheat,* with very elaborate stripes—you know, the kind that *are* actually woven into the fabric. Mom always said to be nice to him because he had a problem but that he was very dear. Whenever I asked what exactly the problem was, she said she'd explain one day when she had appropriate explaining time. When would she have time to explain? I asked. When I got to be about Malcolm's age, she said.

For two years Mr. Dawson had commented upon my growth. This practice ceased the day that I cheerfully commented upon his. Plus, Mr. Dawson was forever trying to sell us products for animals we no longer had, like the Habitrail for the hamster whose final exercise had been a lunge into the kitchen heating duct, or the new tank for our fourteen black mollies (whom I'd inadvertently massacred when I'd attempted to be helpful by cleaning the fish tank with Clorox).

So on this fateful morning Mother had warned me not to say anything about our boa constrictor and to say *only* that we were looking for a mouse.

"Well, Mrs. Warner," said Mr. Dawson, "you've certainly come to the right place. Mice are a specialty here." Gila monsters and Komodo dragons would also have been a specialty if we'd asked. "Right this way, ladies." He smiled and led us over to a wall that spanned some twenty-five feet, against which leaned stacks of tanks, each one filled with mice.

"As you can see, Mrs. W." (my mother hated being called Mrs. W. She also hated people who talked about having a nice day; as she rolled up the car window at the bank drive-thru she would invariably announce that *we'd be having any kind of a day we damn well pleased*) "as regards our *mice,* as I'm sure you've already seen with your own two selves, we've got quite a selection."

He pointed an inky finger toward a nondescript family of light gray mice. "These beauties are Dominican. Over here, ladies, these little gems are *South American reticulated mice.*" He smiled proudly.

"Those black ones are Australian tree mice, quite rare. It all depends what kind of temperament you want. *These are quite playful,"* he said, pointing to a trio of extremely fluffy beige mice. "These guys are super-hearty—they'll live a long time." *Until we get them home,* I thought.

"And this fella," he said, "this little fella's *exceptional!"* Mr. Dawson pointed to a large black-and-white spotted rodent reclining atop some cedar chips. "This is Charlie, our Malaysian bangtail." Mother did not get too close, and despite her blank expression I knew that she was having trouble with the concept of Charlie, the *late* Malaysian bangtail.

"So you see, we've got quite a fantastic selection, as you yourselves can plainly take note. What do you think, Mrs. W.?"

I looked up at Mom, who had winced at his inquiry and was now visibly agitated. She sighed and began to fumble in her pocketbook for what I could only guess was a TicTac, normally produced when she was nervous or seconds before the sermon in church. This composed and genteel woman was clearly rattled, and as she took my hand I noticed hers was shaking a bit. I realized that she, who had endured the deaths of several animals and even more relatives, was now entirely unnerved by the prospect of paying money for something, only to send it willingly to a brutal death by strangulation.

"You know, Mr. Dawson," she said, gathering herself, "I think maybe another time. These are lovely mice, but they're just not *right*. But thanks ever so much for your help."

With that she took my hand and led me quickly out into the sunny and decidedly unmurderous environment of Lancaster Avenue. As we headed down the sidewalk I could tell Mom was trying to figure out how this turn of events would affect me, and I could sense her forming an explanation about death. Or in this case, its avoidance. Suddenly, we heard a voice calling after us. We turned around and saw Mr. Dawson waving manically.

"Wait! Mrs. W.! Hey! Wait! Come back!"

Mother was so horrified by this public display from thirty feet that she pivoted me around and we quickly returned.

"Yes, Mr. Dawson?"

"Well, see, I was thinking that I never asked ya . . . what's the mouse for?"

Mother just stared at him.

"I *mean*," said Mr. Dawson, "is it for a pet, or is it *to eat*?"

After I had spelled *M-i-s-s-i-s-s-i-p-p-i* four times in my head, Mother nodded.

"Well, gosh! Why the heck didn't ya say so? Sure we got those types of mice too. 'Cause you know everybody's gotta eat. Right? You come right this way, ladies!"

And with that we followed him back into the pet shop and he led us all the way to the back and down a flight of rickety stairs, into a musty room that reeked of cigars and sawdust. And at the base of the stairs, across a damp floor, was a large wooden box, about six feet by six feet, inside of which frolicked easily two hundred small white mice. "You shoulda just said so! You want a dozen? They go pretty fast, ya know. And we got ten-ounce rats that'll tide 'em over for a month!" Mr. Dawson was beaming rather satanically at this point. Mother's eyes widened and I felt a little sorry for her. "Well, actually, I think perhaps we'll just start with the one," she said. "Right, dearie?" She looked down at me for some kind of incomprehensible affirmation from an eight-year-old. Mr. Dawson scooped up our hapless mouse by its tail and put it into a box. We followed him upstairs, paid, thanked him, and left.

As we climbed into the car I clutched the box containing this latter-day vestal virgin and we drove home in silence. And never before and never since has the specter of death and guilt been so pronounced for the two of us—although I certainly didn't know it at the time. Because as we headed home all I could think of were the endless opportunities that lay before me in the vast uncharted wilderness of my brother's room.

the fix

· · ·

At first blush, you might not think the late Kurt Cobain and I have a lot in common. Sure, both of us have opposable thumbs and both of us have been spotted with the occasional striped T-shirt. But there's more to it than that.

New York City is the only burg on earth where there may be a certain nobility in being single. And after Clark R. M. Wheeler, M.D., rather unceremoniously returned me for store credit, I elected to move on as best I could, and try to read Dick Francis or something. I never made it to Dick Francis and spent my days in a numb and stupefied state of inertia brought on by the white noise of advertising and my evenings in a numb and stupefied state brought on by gin. Or scotch, whenever I was feeling like Patricia Neal. I even tried to drink bourbon, because then, I reasoned, I could fully appreciate the very Tennessee Williams nature of my despair. I hoped that over the summer I might find myself in a gown at somebody's plantation where I could pitch headfirst over a staircase railing and be done with it. But bourbon made me spit up, and that was even worse. I marveled even then at the human spirit's ability to document its own decay.

Over time my body began actively to participate in this festering gala of gloom, and I soon became quite ill. I started to cough a lot, a condition that I had been taught to ignore. My father was a doctor and, following the adage that cobbler's children wear no shoes, we were never allowed—or really believed—to be sick. Ailments were nothing a good nap or a little Agatha Christie wouldn't take care of; if one persisted, we should simply take a tub and forget about it. Thus I ignored the cough. Racking chest spasms, too, seemed to me merely a punishment for dumping a devoted investment banker a few years prior. I started losing weight, which was fine by me. My skin, which had dictated the duration of every tropical vacation my family ever took when I was a child (as every doctor had diagnosed me a melanoma waiting to happen), became even more pale. I could have sung in some Cure cover band. Still, I did nothing.

It was also true that I had gone to a boarding school where getting sick was something we'd all learned to master with extreme sophistication. In the ninth grade, upperclassmen showed us how to correctly hold a thermometer against a lightbulb to create the desired effect without producing an unusual rush of mercury (to which we knew the nurses had become wise). In the tenth grade we were taught how to put just enough Blistex in our eyes to make them appear blood-shot and teary without permanently damaging the iris or cornea. Six or seven cinnamon Red Hots could be cooked over a heating coil with grape soda, which, gargled with, at the right temperature, would produce a permanent reddening stain throughout the tongue and gum area, landing one in the infirmary for an entire afternoon. Alka Seltzer, peanut butter, and 7-Up, shaken and shotgunned through a water bottle, would produce the requisite intestinal carnage for an entire weekend spent luxuriating before the nurse's watchful eye and her twenty-seven-inch television.

In fact, everything at school was formulaic. We lived with a black market somewhat akin to any number of correctional facilities. Alcohol was stored inside ceiling panels, or more securely inside the bathroom heating vent, which could be opened in a flash with the straight edge of a dime. The booze was procured by one of my roommates (there were four girls to a room), a rather promiscuous, tattooed girl who had ridden on and claimed to "know about" motorcycles. It was she who explained to us that the Marrakesh Express was probably something other than an African transport system, and she became our pipeline to the "outside" when we needed liquor. For a cut of the bounty, she would perform any number of lurid sex acts upon the night watchman atop one of the tables in the school's formal dining room, which was directly beneath us. The guard then happily purchased as much liquor as we wanted and delivered the post-fornication quarry to a mutually agreed-upon checkpoint broom closet.

But rather than prolong this manic digression, I will say simply that it was now years later, and I was quite sick, and so emotionally despondent that the hair on my head was oddly *sore,* and I was curling up like a nautilus or an attacked beetle whenever I was alone. I would wander the streets underneath my own personal black cloud. On Sundays I was careful to avoid certain residential neighborhoods where happy couples in each other's collegiate sweatshirts roughhoused carelessly en route to their favorite bagel repository. I have always found Manhattan's Upper West Side very arrogant, with its self-satisfied brownstones and cagily proud inhabitants, all of whom seemed eager to prove that they could buy their favorite imported pasta, purchase tasteful chenille throw pillows, locate prime decompressed espresso beans and egg-white gelato, find Peruvian handmade picture frames, aerobically climb Mount Everest, and have their Rollerblades sharpened *all on the very same block,* all in about three minutes. Of course I was sure these same hateful truths existed on the Upper East Side. Only there one had far more places to consume food (with your attractive start-up-website-designer boyfriend who only *welcomed* your clothing tips) than to actually work that romantic and dewy-eyed meal off.

I struggled to see the bright side but couldn't. And I have never really been able to get behind that Be Thankful for Situations You Aren't In, Diseases You Don't Have, Jobs You Didn't Lose, Dictatorships You Didn't Have to Live Under thing. Yes, it makes sense, but you just plain *didn't,* so why be grateful? The big *whew* never feels that good when you've got that black heart and the empty life.

Then one morning I actually fainted in my office in the Time & Life Building. Although I happened to be seated, so there was little drama. I was taken to the company nurse, a small woman with the requisite false warmth, nude panty hose, and facial hair found in most middle-school medical professionals. She asked me to go lie down, as I was obviously ill, and I succumbed to her ministering until I was lucid enough to realize that I was an adult with my own home, to which I would flee just as soon as I stopped seeing four of everything. Before releasing me she gave me a prescription for some cough syrup, and I shoved it into a pocket before racing out of the Time & Life infirmary.

The following evening, wobbly, nauseous, and exhausted, I made myself attend a party. I went because everybody told me no matter what else I did in my depressed, anguished postbreakup state, I was to (a) categorically avoid all country music; (b) shun anything to do with Lionel Richie; and (c) attend each and every gathering to which I was invited, whether I behaved like a zombie or not. This particular shindig was in an aggressively sanctimonious brownstone off Columbus Avenue. Decorated in that annoying way that suggests that the height of city living is to be beamed into some pine and Navajo Indian–patterned fishing lodge filled with candles and hand-wrought knickknacks. *Why it's our own private Adirondack fishing camp on Seventy-eighth Street!* Where you are expected to get excited about a rocking chair, and where you're supposed to smile appreciatively at a *throw* . . . a throw that is simply and exactly that—not purchased to cover anything or keep anyone warm while sleeping. And the *brick*. The ubiquitous, bewilderingly coveted "exposed brick." I suddenly wondered which clothes some random emperor had been sporting when he took a shine to this inexplicable wall-covering phenomenon. Why? Why were we required to marvel at the appearance of a solid wall of bricks *indoors* that by all rights no one would bat an eyelash at were it outdoors, covering a home, where it belonged?

This is one of the reasons why I like only antiseptic, white-noisy high-rise apartments and hotels. I've always known down deep that I'll spend my days living inside a multiple-dwelling structure—always with a uniformed man between me and the rest of the world. I am, and have always been, this side of assisted living.

My host was one of my best friends, a gay fashion-magazine editor whom I'd known forever and who was wonderfully comforting. He'd been away for the previous six months compiling "must-have" luxury-item lists for his ravenous readers (who would all immediately acquire an Indonesian atoll if he so directed). And since I'd exhausted the required grace period during which everyone else is required to let you whinge without telling you to "shut up because you know it's over and you'll never get him back," I knew I still had a bonus grief voucher which I could thoughtfully exercise that evening with him. Unfortunately, I'd forgotten that for all his acute insight and verbal dexterity, he was also the one person who, when subjects like these came up, would simply remark that "fellas are shits and that's all" before putting his head across my breast and making a sad cooing sound. More of my pals arrived and commented appreciatively upon the various antiquities strewn throughout Matthew's tasteful home, and before long I was happily engaged in a heady and important discussion about Olympics steroid use, people we knew who had actually played Stratego, the suspiciousness of the Dead Sea Scrolls, and the nuclear fission required to produce Lay's new fat-free potato chips. At about eleven o'clock, however, I could feel myself starting to slip into a Russian stupor of grief. And thus, cold sober, coughing badly, and convinced of life's meaninglessness (or at least my own life's meaninglessness), I drifted home to read. When I returned to my apartment I located the Time Inc. cough syrup, which sat unopened on top of my icebox. I took a tablespoonful, put on a nightie, and crawled into bed with eight plump, juicy, relevant magazines.

And that's when it started to happen.

It was imperceptible at first, but then it grew. And how. As I read I suddenly began to feel love and a deep compassion. I became conscious of a new, deeper appreciation of Steven Spielberg's inner conflicts. I welled up over a tiny kitten that had been rescued by an Appalachian fireman. I became passionately outraged over the Native American Plight. I began to tear up about strife in the Sudan. I felt visceral anger toward all the publicity people who had ever betrayed Nicole Kidman, Corey Feldman, or Corey Haim. I blazed with sympathy over Justin Timberlake's privacy-free existence. *Suddenly everything I read meant the world to me.* In one instant I was wholly conscious of a deeper connection to anyone whose life appeared in headline form. A fireball of acute empathy smoldered painfully in my heart. I put the

magazine down and knew that more than anything else, I
needed to write thank-you notes to everyone who had ever
been kind to me, who had ever undertaken a thoughtful
task, who had ever supported me in any way. I hopped out
of bed and rummaged around for some good stationery.
Then I realized that thank-you notes would never be
enough. No. What I should really do was *phone* people and
tell them just how loved they were. How appreciated. These
people really and truly needed to know about the love. Then
I noticed it was one o'clock in the morning and that it
wouldn't be very considerate to call, even if it was to show that
love. No, that wouldn't do. And then it dawned upon me
that I would send everyone I knew flowers. Great, huge bas-
kets of flowers when they weren't expecting any—enormous
sentinels of affection to brighten their days, so they'd know
somebody *really really* cared. Which I did. My love was bound-
less and full, and I wanted only to reach out to everyone I'd
ever met and say, *Thanks, you know, you're terrific!* As I was thumbing through the phone book seeking out the FTD florist's
800 number, I suddenly felt light-headed. I went and lay
down, only to drift into a deep sleep.

When I awoke, some sixteen hours later, I felt rested and
curiously exhausted at the same time. I looked at the magazines strewn across my bed and couldn't really remember
what had happened the night before, except that I recalled
being gripped by a terrible desire to write hundreds of
thank-you notes to tell everyone that I really and truly loved
them more than words could ever reveal. Of course now, in
the daylight, I had no such desire whatsoever and was hor-

rified that I'd even entertained the notion of sending flowers to more than thirty people. It then dawned on me that I
hadn't slept so deeply in years.

That evening, before I went to bed, I took another tablespoon of cough syrup while sitting at the computer. Within
the course of about ten minutes I was scrolling furiously
through my e-mail addresses, firing off missives—*"Just to say
hi cause I was thinkin about ya!"*—to every person in my database.
Some people received "What's up? It's been too long!!!"
followed by yards of *x*'s and *o*'s to bear my newfound adora-
tion. I was thrilled. Completely buoyed by mankind and by
my extraordinary good fortune to be alive. Buoyed by life
itself. I even wanted to phone Clark R. M. Wheeler, M.D.,
and say that all was forgiven, that cheating was human and
life was short.

Within a month my cough was gone, and so was my newfound cough syrup. I had taken a tablespoon about once or
twice a week, whenever I needed a little pick-me-up. Suddenly, the question became where to get more, and since
my father had died, I no longer had instant access to prescription drugs. (Not that I'd ever been interested in
procuring anything other than swimmer's ear ointment
from him anyway.) So a few weeks later I asked my uncle, a
soothing and kindly Christian physician who would have
been the constable or the vicar in any Dickens novel, if
he could refill my prescription. "Of course, little lady," he
said. "Glad to help." I took a pint of the serum home the
next day. Over the course of the next year I would indulge
in my tiny habit—only a tablespoon and never with any al-

cohol in my system—before I went to bed. But I was aware and I was an adult. I was no addict. Nor had I ever liked any drugs to date. I could stop any time I wanted. This much I knew.

The following fall, *Come as You Are*, the harrowing and, some argued, definitive book about Nirvana, was published, and I devoured it as I did any book with limited editorial and lots of facts and pictures. One evening I came to a chapter about Kurt's drug abuse. It explained, quite lucidly, how whenever he was unable to "score" more "smack" he would simply medicate himself with the Hycodan hydrate—which was *my cough syrup*—"stolen from other junkies like him." In fact, musicians, roadies, and others in the know casually referred to it as Blue Velvet. Shocked, I raced immediately into my kitchen and poured the contents of my own deadly stash down the sink. Never again did I toy with what had been, I thought, such a harmless infatuation with a syrup that made me want to write thank-you notes to everyone I'd ever met. Never again, I vowed, would I fiddle with fate in such a careless way, edging as I had been closer toward the precipice of addiction and ultimately, I was sure, a most violent and unpleasant death. There would be no Requiem for a Nice Girl. No way. I'd get clean.

From that moment on, when I slid into a depressive abyss, I was able to rationalize to myself that, unlike Kurt, no matter how bad it got it was still a good kind of bad.

oedipus t. rex

· · ·

My eminently low-key psychiatrist father had a patient who, for six years, insisted that she'd been savagely impregnated by the Prince of Wales. Repeatedly. When I asked Dad if this was true, he explained that, in fact, it wasn't.

"So does that mean she's lying?" I asked.

"Well, not exactly," my father said, hoping that was sufficient and that I would not press on. He then returned to one of his many yellow legal pads, in whose domain he was far more comfortable writing than he was explaining the psychosexual fantasy disorders of his patients (and members of England's royal family) to his nine-year-old daughter.

I would note for the purposes of psychiatric confidentiality that all of us knew about this alleged ravishing *only* because she phoned our house daily and, rather than just leave a message, identified herself as the Prince's sometime paramour. And mother of his child.

"Well, was she impregnated or not?" I pushed.

"Not entirely. Mrs. Willoughby doesn't actually *know* the Prince of Wales," he said, looking exasperated.

"So then she's lying," I persisted. "Dad, does she *like* to lie? Is lying her thing?"

"Well, actually, it's a fantasy," he said, squinting and realizing he'd pitched us both headfirst into yet another gopher hole of supercomplicated inquiry.

"Okay, so what's fantasy?" I inquired, and he removed the pencil from behind his ear and began to examine it. I watched him search its Ticonderoga No. 2 logo for some kind of answer. Locating no Truth there, he methodically reached for his *Physicians' Desk Reference*. When he realized that very little of the *PDR*'s content would answer my annoying but possibly legitimate questions, he put the tome down and considered defining the word *fantasy*. He regarded me as seriously as he could, which may have been difficult, considering my outfit. For one thing, I had taken to decorating my enormous flesh-colored corrective eye patch. Today it was festooned with feathers, decals, and glitter, in what may have been an early homage to Marc Bolan and T. Rex. Who could be sure? I was also sporting my favorite Day-Glo orange-and-black tiger-striped bodysuit, and my brother's men's size 12 Jack Purcells, for no apparent reason at all. Plus, I happened to be wearing an enormous cape fashioned from a Pan American Airlines beach towel. And now my father had to define *fantasy* within the context of "psychosexual disorder."

He cleared his throat and said, "Well, Miss Pink, let's see."

And I leaned in toward him, the motion causing some of the gluey glitter to flake off my eye patch and land in my open, wondering mouth. I spat it out silently and affixed my gaze on my father.

"A fantasy is when you really, really want something to happen"—he paused—"a lot."

"Like Christmas?" I asked.

"Kind of like Christmas," he answered.

I asked why the patient in question didn't just *ask Santa* if he could please arrange for the Prince of Wales to impregnate her at Christmas. He squinted again with that exasperated look, the look that said everything. The look that years later I would recognize as signifying a kind of departure on his part. The look that reaffirmed my suspicions that he'd never, ever, really been comfortable with children. Not because he didn't like them—he certainly loved us—but because he didn't have any idea what to do with them.

"I suppose Santa doesn't know the Prince of Wales."

"No?"

"Not well." He rubbed his forehead, probably wondering about the wisdom behind proposing a de facto Santa Claus in relation to psychosexual fantasy. And then he said, "That's why. So why don't you go out and drum up some fun, kiddo? Why don't you go for a swim or check the bird feeder or something," he said absentmindedly, returning to his papers.

"Dad, I can't."

"Why?"

"Dad, I can't go swim."

"Hmm? Why not?"

"*Dad,*" I said, and he looked up.

I pointed to the window, and we both looked out. And there, busily under way, was one of the worst hailstorms to overtake Philadelphia's Main Line. It was the middle of January.

"Oh . . . look at that. Well, gosh. Say, maybe Malcolm would play bocce with you in the hallway." This was a horrifying enough idea to send me on my way, since my sixteen-year-old brother Malcolm and I liked neither each other nor the game of bocce. With that I marched out of Dad's office in my own cloud of glitter and feathers, my cape spanning majestically out behind me, to forage for food or greet one of Dad's patients who would be parked in the driveway. I happily spent that afternoon developing my own rather elaborate Christmas "fantasy," wherein Malcolm might experience a spontaneous explosion though the walls of his stomach—until such time as he was forced to return my Barbie, her hapless sister, Skipper, and the Malibu camper he'd boldly abducted days prior.

And of course, because it was the 1970s, my dad saw about half of his patients in his office at our house. Patients who were, unless my father got to them first, often mine to greet and welcome, frequently in period costume. Thus, Dr. Warner's psychiatric patients often encountered a nine-year-old medieval wench, often with two of our golden retrievers attired in T-shirts. On another day they might be greeted by a cheetah with an eye patch, along with our cat, whom I often draped across my shoulders like a tabby boa. I had been told to usher patients into our living room, where they would sit, and I would then suggest they take a crack at one of the puzzles we always had out for them on a Lucite table. Or they could sip the warm iced tea I brought them and stare at one of our many mid-1970s Vasarely prints, until such time as either one of these products made them dizzy.

I learned that my father had died on voice mail. I know that your parents, once they get used to the fact that you have a nice antiseptic desk job with wonderful gadgetry like voice mail, soon figure out that it's private and that you'll check it immediately because it might be a boy or pizza or something. And to that end, parents also realize that they can now chatter away aimlessly into it, as if they were talking to you. In real time. In fact it's even better than when they're talking to you, because you can't interrupt. So voice mail is really just a better, quieter, more available child, and they robustly throw themselves into its confidence. This is what my mother does. Or did, when I had a fancy job with all the technical accoutrements associated with being a writer on the thirtieth floor of Rockefeller Center's Time & Life Building.

So you've been working for five years (nor will you find out—until it's way too late—that what you thought was work wasn't really work at all), and then you get into the golden *why bother with dry cleaners* haze associated with your sixth year, and the endless lunch and shopping outings to get yourself through the seventh year, until your eighth year when you suddenly find yourself scheduling meetings with clients after eleven-thirty not because you aren't in your office yet but because you'll need at least an hour to catch up with all the people you chattered and smoked with the night before. And this is ten years ago, long before anybody cared about apple martinis or global villages. You'll need that hour of post-mortem catch-up to chatter about nothing at all, to rehear that nobody likes where they are, and how close you all are to putting a pistol to your temple. When in fact none of you will do any such thing until one horrifying day when some-one you know, not well but well enough, actually *does* do this. At which point you and everyone else clear your throats, feel shame, and think, *Wow, I've got it pretty good,* and *What an awful wake-up call*—until a month later when you all go right back to commiserating and thinking you're abundantly average.

So I was on my office phone talking to maybe four peo-ple in a sort of strange but common tele—round robin, and I had two message lights blinking and I checked one and it was somebody nice asking me if perhaps I'd forgotten to pay my Visa bill for thirteen weeks, and then the other phone call was Mom. They'd been on vacation and were staying in a cottage in Carmel. And she said that the night before, after the orchestra, they'd gone off to bed and that at about four-fifteen that morning Dad had sat up in bed, coughed several times, and then slumped over and lain still. She'd called EMS and they'd come immediately and had managed to resuscitate his heart but nothing else was functioning, and they had rushed him to a big hospital in San Jose, Cali-fornia, where I hope I will never, ever, ever, have to go.

My father had perfectly symmetrical features and a nice square jaw, but he was entirely unaware of the way he looked. He was one of those men who was always kind of shy—and possibly startled by his looks—like an ordinary person who completely unknowingly happens to have a spectacular array of roses in his hand at all times. He always wore dark tweed blazers and gray flannel pants and loafers, and rep ties attached to his button-down with a tiny monogrammed golden disc that my mother had engraved, and replaced, every year. And during the six-week period between his losing the gold tie clip and its replacement, Dad would keep his ties affixed to his shirts with a paper clip.

He was smart, patient, and cautiously optimistic about almost everything. He was also pathologically devoted to Princeton, Sigmund Freud, and suburban Chicago.

I remember wanting him to be someone else. Anybody else. Because when you're in the third grade or the seventh grade or even the ninth grade and everyone else has fathers with names like Bill or Jack or Bob, you don't want a father with a name like Silas. And when there's a tiny blank on a form and the other kids write down "stockbroker" or "lawyer" or just "businessman" there, you don't want to write "psychiatrist." And when it says *employer* and you have been taught to write "self," you vow never, ever, to go work for that queer, singular, and positively uncool Self Company. And when other kids have fathers who are driving one regular car and then a Porsche on the weekend or maybe they've got a Galaxie 500 tucked away in the garage and they tinker with it, and you say, *Dad, why do you drive a leased Oldsmobile Delta 88 and why do you get a new one every two years and what's cool about that, and he says there's nothing cool. It works. I work. And I'm not cool*—that can also be rather disheartening.

Then there was the week Brenda Frink announced in the lunchroom that her father was about to take SmithKline Laboratories public. And that week *my* father was giving a talk at the University of Pennsylvania about Gender Disorder and Impotence in Adolf Hitler, John Wayne Gacy, and Franklin Roosevelt. This is not cool when you're twelve.

I learned about sex from my dad. He never knew it, though. I was about ten, and reading just fine. Whenever my parents were away, which they were frequently, I would rummage through his office for an issue of his *Journal of the American Medical Association.* These were dull, but then I discovered the closest thing I ever got to real porn: the magazine *Human Sexuality.* It was rife with dozens of photographs of genitalia, and I would eagerly pore through and read. What I didn't know was that said genitals were all somehow disfigured, diseased, or essentially being shown to illustrate an unfortunate condition. Even the *before* and *after* shots riveted me, because the before pictures always featured somebody's infected, enlarged, and oozing bad part, while the after photo was only a slightly less infected oozing bad part. Thus, when other kids referred to "fooling around" or "making out," I was quick to inquire whether someone might be frigid or displaying Oedipal tendencies or latent homoerotic fantasies. I am fairly certain that, as I sat on the bleachers of the Haverford School football field kissing

Billy Gardner and then hearing him talking about his "johnson," my queries about his "nocturnal emissions" possibly affecting his "erectile tissue" were not so welcome. Then I found Dad's copy of *Everything You Always Wanted to Know About Sex (but Were Afraid to Ask)* from 1969, and I was off and running. Soon I was an expert on the dizzying, hypnotic effect of noncontact erotic foreplay on males and how to remove lightbulbs, myriad vegetables, and garden tools from one's nether regions without membrane damage. And this is how I learned about sex, long before any discussion of birds and bees came to the table. And of course when that discussion did come up, it all seemed rather bland. Because who cares what happens if two people really really love each other when there could actually be bondage, frigidity, fetish hormones, and genital mutilation brought on by chromosomally induced psychotic episodes? That's where I wanted to be.

My dad encouraged inquiry and all kinds of intellectual investigation, which none of us thought was cool, and he always felt that kids should be presented with a broad spectrum of information—and that we would grow to discern and appreciate life's complexities. When my parents' friend Tom Brookshier, our local sportscaster, and his wife invited my parents to go see *Blazing Saddles* with them, along with their daughter and me, Mother murmured something to him and Dad said, "I suspect it'll sail cinematically over their heads. They probably won't get it." And of course we didn't get one bit. In 1970, when Dad and Mother took six of the children from their combined marriages to Europe, he adopted a similar attitude. He said he thought it was important for the children to see Dachau. I remember my mother murmuring again, and then Dad turning to her in the car and saying, "She probably won't understand much of it. But what she does get, I hope, will sink in."

In a professorial way my dad was as absentminded as he was spontaneous—especially with purchases. For example, after college, when I began to write copy, I was absolutely consumed by all things marketing, advertising, or brand-oriented. I was fascinated to the point of obsession with the media. And Christmas 1989 I remember being blown away when I opened a present from him whose title was *Total Media: The Thinking Person's Guide to Media Immersion.* I was shocked and delighted that he really understood what made me tick. Absolutely thrilled that he had noticed, listened, and remembered. Until I opened the book up and discovered that this was in fact a guide to another kind of media—featuring huge color photos and exhaustive text on how to arrange your stereo, VCR, and CD system. I never told him about the book's contents, because he was like that in bookshops, an impulsive buyer who didn't always check.

The reason I'm bringing him up is because a few weeks ago, I was in a bookshop in New York, feeling smug because I was in a bookshop in New York, when I came upon a book called *My Incredible Life with the Westies,* which I immediately scooped up without even glancing through and purchased, delighted that I could send my mother a little book about her beloved fluffy white Scottish terriers. And this morning

Mom phoned to thank me for sending her *My Incredible Life with the Westies.* And when she told me that the book was not about fluffy white dogs at all, rather it was a violent account of one person's undercover work inside New York's most brutal Irish gangs, I realized in a teensy but not queer and Harry Chapinlike way, I'd turned out a bit like my dad after all.

hallowed grind

. . .

I didn't know much about Los Angeles, but what I didn't know I didn't like. Although I did have one last business trip to make for Time Inc. and decided that I might as well go and see the place, and it would also be a chance to stay with two of my oldest and dearest friends, who had rather inexplicably decided to live there. So I went.

Mary and Jed Dillon live in that actors' shtetl just south of Melrose Avenue, a few blocks west of Hollywood. It's a quiet neighborhood where, in spite of its quaintness, one sees a fair amount of demi-recognizable up-and-comers. The evening I arrived they took me to a dinner party at a house in the Hollywood Hills, and it was nice because there were several friendly dogs and a seemingly unlimited supply of pistachios. We were greeted by several elfin embryonic girls who had clearly been airlifted in from Urban Outfitters. Our hostess was a strikingly beautiful production designer married to one of those men who knows a little too much about fennel and cumin, but it gives him the legitimacy to put the FREE TIBET bumper sticker on his Land Rover and reference NPR a lot.

Jed and Mary speculated that everyone had surmised I was a writer either because I was wearing glasses, using polysyllables, or shrouding my chest. They weren't sure which.

"You still really like New York?" Mary asked me, handing me four Doritos.

"How could you not?" I said.

"But L.A. is awfully nice. Things happen here."

True. Things did happen there. Things for entertainment types. Which I was decidedly not. Or for compelling people like Mary, who are just sort of *touched*. Perhaps the kindest person I know, Mary can find the upside in a paper cut. At first I had found her goodness suspect; now I am certain I am wildly lucky to have her in my life. She hadn't liked New York, it was true, but I couldn't fault her. Just because I couldn't even begin to imagine living anywhere else didn't mean that she didn't have some strange, incomprehensible reasons for wanting to leave. Her husband, Jed, is a smart and very skilled painter with little tolerance for dull or initiative-free people. He does not suffer even one single fool. Mary is taller, prettier, and considerably nicer than I will ever be. She has a children's craft show on some random cable-television station, inadvertently titled *Make It with Me*. Due to this title, Mary has been an obscure and totally misunderstood cable-TV sex symbol ever since. With weird fan e-mails to prove it. And all she ever really wanted to do was be an after-school program coordinator for 'tweens.

We gazed over at several people milling about with margaritas in their tanned, carefree hands. I marveled at the Hollywood Hills bungalow in which we sat. It was a superb little gem, nestled in eucalyptus, camouflaged like some rare California marsupial. Once inside, you'd never have known that you were probably less than thirty-six inches from the Oscar nominee eating a colonically approved gluten meal in the hacienda next door. Nor, when lazing atop its many sun-flecked muslin ottomans, would you know that you were in a home whose security system could effectively monitor (and probably communicate with) missiles traveling through the atmosphere. Because you'd be too busy engaged in a breezy discussion about the upcoming Georgia O'Keeffe biopic, the state of national siege brought on by an afternoon's drizzle, the ubiquity of earthquakes, the ubiquity of Jennifer Garner, and the cultural horrorscape that is Santa Barbara. And then there was the sun.

I entered the kitchen, and the wall of sound that greeted me was hardly new. Everywhere good-looking men who were about to return to careers in house painting blithely offered up grains of truth to quivering anemic girls, and vice versa. To my left: "They fucked that film up with the editing." Dead ahead: "They're gonna make people try and survive on a desert island? No way is anyone gonna watch." Down center: "I love that lipstick . . . wait—is that *magic pout, ruby, cuckold,* or *alarm*?" To my right: "Sorry about your pilot." Ten o'clock: "The 'Boulevard of Broken Dreams' one *is* Sunset, right?"

As people began to discuss the six-headed hydra that is Los Angeles street parking, I took in facts about this sprawling, lease-based city with its buzzing, frequently clogged streets. Apparently, Fountain is the smart man's Sunset. And Willoughby is the thinking man's Fountain. Romaine is the cautious man's Willoughby, and San Vicente doesn't really go anywhere at all. The people dining at Swingers, aren't. When someone tells you they're "shopping a screenplay," this just means that they own a computer. And if a woman tells you she's a "stylist," she is actually between jobs.

In the living room I was swept into a tragically earnest discussion about books. Tragic because I don't read. Nor had I rented any of what was being discussed. A kindly, balding man offered me a joint, which I declined, the rejection of which is always difficult because no matter how old you are, how successful you are, or how cool you are, there's still no way to say no to pot without reminding everyone watching you of some 1979 ABC Afterschool Special about the Awkward Girl. So I simply explain that I'd "already gotten baked that afternoon."

A skinny website wizard in leather who had clearly never laundered anything besides maybe money pointedly asked me which books I liked as a kid. As I scooped up and swallowed a handful of sage and tea-tree potpourri, I said, "The usual stuff."

"I know girls like you," he said. "You always like Henry James." He winked at me, obviously some kind of tacit acknowledgment of my velvet-corset fetish.

At that moment Mary appeared and waved me over, emphatically introducing me to a blond guy she'd just met. She then announced that both he and I hailed from *the exact same place. Where?* I wondered. *Hades?*

It turned out this guy really *had* grown up outside of Philadelphia. I focused for a second. The blond guy smiled.

"I'm Walter Kimball. Didn't you go to Haverford Friends School?"

I was astounded. I managed to smile and bleat, "Yes, I think so . . ." while I groped around for a cigarette, in the process knocking a huge cup of beer onto the shiny product-laden scalps of six young girls seated Indian-style next to an interactive CD-ROM Ouija board. I certainly did know this guy. And how.

I wondered if there was any color left in my face. Then I wondered if there was any lipstick left on my lips.

Walter was curious to know what I'd been up to. He confessed that he hadn't remembered me at first, however once he saw me I was unmistakable. *But in a good way,* he assured me. Meanwhile I stared somewhat stupidly at him, stunned by the fact that this was the very man who, twenty-six years earlier, had caused me to start writing in the first place. Although he didn't know it. As he headed off to the bar to get drinks, my mind reeled.

Walter Kimball. He was blond. That's all you could say. Very, very blond. And he'd smiled—that *winning* smile. The kind of all-county all-state smile the hopes and dreams of a small town eventually get pinned on. He'd had a prepubescent charisma. He'd dressed in the fashion favored by most second-graders, and while no child was unique or characterized by a deep sense of style, he had always looked *right*. Every day he'd worn a striped shirt whose bands were so precise, whose background was so rich—be it buttery yellow or sky blue or a crispy Clorox white—that he'd resonated purity and virtue.

Our encounters had always been brief. A simple nod of approbation when I had secured a particularly large cicada in a mayonnaise jar, or maybe brief eye contact when I relinquished both grape- and orange-scented Magic Markers to him. Nor in the second grade was there much opportunity for witty banter or comment.

But alas, I had been quite gangly, and my front teeth extended well beyond the others—in fact it would be another ten years before a visionary dentist was able to bevel them down a quarter of an inch. My right leg, due to a botched IV hookup to remedy infant spinal meningitis, was literally bent, midcalf. A two-inch platform had been added to the sole of one of my red oxfords to correct the imbalance. My eyes were perilously close together, and if that wasn't enough, I had also just been diagnosed with a severe wandering eye. They told me I'd need to wear a corrective patch. This was okay, I thought, a patch can kind of be cool—like a pair of crutches invariably are for about the first seven minutes. However, I also had a very pronounced astigmatism in the other eye. That meant a patch *plus* corrective lenses. Okay. So for one day I wore pink tortoiseshell glasses with a reasonably cool black plastic shield over one lens. The following day the black plastic shield was brutally shattered at dodgeball. My ophthalmologist then announced that I'd need something *more permanent.* For three years thereafter I arrived at school with one lens of my glasses completely blacked out with sticky masking tape.

And young Walter Kimball, while never cruel, had not been particularly interested in discovering my many complicated inner workings. So I had agonized over how to get his pure blond attention.

How? How could I ever be noticed, my myriad physical shortcomings overlooked or even embraced? Then one morning, seated at the kitchen counter, I had a shattering realization. First, I reasoned that people like people whom everybody else likes. Now, Walter, though worshipped and admired by me, was not *that* well known in school. And it occurred to me that *nobody* is above a personal-ratings boost. That's when it hit me. *If I could make Walter Kimball the most popular man in school, he would naturally, in his deep gratitude, want me for his own.* If he were "it," then I would become *itesque* for putting him there. The question then became *How could I make Walter Kimball an icon?*

Then it came to me. I'd write a play.

At the time we were learning in science about the arctic tundra. With the polar ice cap as backdrop, I would, I reasoned, bring its many inhabitants to theatrical life in a play. Suddenly my class, which consisted of some fifteen children, began to take shape before my eyes. Or eye. One by one I went through each and every child, and based upon their physical characteristics—and more important, my affinity for him or her—each child was assigned a role. Kiera Liensbacher, a pretty and athletic girl who looked down on me, became a burrowing Atlantic vole, a tiny nocturnal shrew who would quickly be felled by a predator. Reggie King, a hyperactive child who made other children nervous but not me so much, became a snow lynx. Beth Keating and Kim Ashwood—noisy, gossipy do-gooders—quickly became mindless, spinstery puffins. Finally it came time for my crowning achievement: parts for Walter Kimball and me. Now, anyone who knew anything in Mrs. Danziger's science class knew that the most important, indeed the most powerful, feared, and respected of the tundra community was the Kodiak bear. The role model for all other animals. With no known predator. Thus, I immediately cast Walter and myself as a pair of Kodiak bears. We were king and queen over all we surveyed.

The world premiere of my masterpiece was performed at the annual parents' picnic, held beneath the school's mock orange tree. The parents and children of all six grades attended, and everyone sat rapt as our arctic extravaganza unfolded. My own parents were shocked at what I'd done for love. Naturally, our little thespic masterpiece was a huge success.

And having watched enough episodes of *The Andy Williams Show* and *Lawrence Welk,* I knew to take Walter's hand at the end of the performance as we bowed, thus sealing our bond forever. It absolutely did the trick, and Walter was over at our house the very next afternoon, where we shared a romantic stroll to the Radnor Pharmacy and were permitted to charge twenty-five cents' worth of candy apiece. Later that evening, after I had spit up the eighteen ounces of licorice I'd ingested, I ruminated happily on the fact that I was finally Walter's girlfriend, his costar, and his agent. The following month he dumped me, himself having succumbed to the dark Sicilian charms of Heather Ann Garzerelli, a satanic pixie know-it-all whose IQ automatically split in half when boys were near. But by that time I was able to adapt, since three kids had already commissioned scripts from me and the local Oldsmobile dealer was forking over $1.25 every other week if I would come up with four new words for his son.

When the mature Walter Kimball returned from the bar he was just as gracious as when he'd left—it was I who had made this tiny journey in my mind and who received him now with a sense of relief and a strange sort of accomplishment. He couldn't have been nicer, was entirely devoid of artistic pretense, and seemed to remember nothing of my palsied goonishness. He was intelligent and articulate and admitted that he was as uncomfortable in Los Angeles as I was, even though he actually lived there.

"It's weird, but I guess you can't ever really escape the Main Line," he said resolutely.

At that moment my sense that I was going nowhere fast on some kind of Protestant monorail to doom evaporated. Because some strange ghost had popped out of nowhere and had inexplicably made me realize that I was still growing up, that I had an awfully long way to go, but that there was something linear in life. That perhaps it wasn't so bad after all. And perhaps even Los Angeles wasn't as bad as I had initially imagined. And that maybe I was just griping because I could.

grievous bodily charm

. . .

And so I had been seized by a somewhat crippling depression marked by my inability to do much more on a daily basis than bathe and smoke. It was possible my job *was* becoming genuinely poisonous, and maybe working in direct mail did make me the Devil's Letter Carrier. But then again, I wasn't making pornography or performing vivisection; I just happened to do a marketing persuading thing remarkably well and I was enjoying a modicum of success.

Meanwhile, my pals were starting to marry and spawn and talk about mortgages, guest towels, and cholesterol. They'd all begun to watch a lot of A&E. I'd begun to drink a lot of Tanqueray. I am pretty sure I was headed down the toxic garden path of Mrs. Howell. Suddenly my midtown co-op held all the appeal of a toe abscess. Five hundred ninety-two square feet of promise became simply a place where I could remain fetal and undisturbed. I began to snap at people gloomily and miserably like some injured Russian terrier.

Mother said, "Maybe a little break would do you some

good" in that way that meant she thought I was beginning to eye ovens, shotguns, and bell towers. "Why not just get away from it all, Lambchop?" she asked. "With any luck, you'll return as a fully two-dimensional person."

Even my psychotherapist agreed, making it not just a personal matter but a medical one as well. My family seemed to feel that some leisure might actually be *in order,* and since I knew they typically viewed me as a bonbon-consuming, grounds-strolling, topiary garden–viewing idiot, this must, then, be serious.

So I'd take a vacation.

Trevor Graham was a friend and playwright who had, like me, ridden horses as a child. Needless to say, within New York's arty downtown theatrical community and its healthily liberal magazine world, there is rarely an appropriate time to recount one's past fox-hunting experiences. Not that I chose to, since I now regard it as an entirely barbaric sport. But the past is just that, and Trevor and I had built a heady friendship on our shared secret childhood activities. Now we rode for fun, about once a decade.

So I phoned him, and next thing I knew, we'd booked a horseback-riding trip in the Scottish Highlands. Technically called a "pony trek," it was neither. Both of us felt ourselves quite competent with horses, so we had requested the most dangerous route we could find. The travel agent found us what they called the "Braveheart Highland Sojourn." Cool. In fact, we were warned that this particular ride had proven fatal to a pair of intrepid riders the year before, due to Scotland's deadly peat bogs. *Even better.* Naturally, we were thrilled and just as arrogant as we could be. We still felt safe, because you always believe there's something very soft and civilized about Europe. Besides, we learned, we would be hosted by a duchess, one Ilse Duchamps Fontaine-Maddox, a Belgian royal who had married a philandering English duke in the fifties, who now owned about six million acres in Scotland. This trip involved riding many miles by day, then staying in some of Scotland's cutest and quaintest inns by night.

On the flight over, Trevor and I struggled desperately to extract nourishment from the nine dry-roasted peanuts we'd been awarded as coach travelers. We whiled away the hours wondering how much they pay the actors in the emergency-landing videos, and at what age men decide to become flight stewards, living out of small wheeled bags.

At the Glasgow airport we noticed other Americans on the trip, who greeted us raucously. The middle-aged Minnesota couple in matching ten-gallon hats and buckskin leather vests. The tiny lesbian holistic-medicine dealer/ dressage expert from Napa, bearing dozens of photographs of her newborn daughter—arrived at via artificial insemination.

All I could think was *There must be some mistake.* Why were we traveling with these nether-dwelling simians who wouldn't know angst or irony if they were soaking in it? Trevor told me to shut up and cheerily asked where our Lake Wobegon friends had purchased their full Western regalia (Best Buy), and how the tiny lesbian had come to settle upon the right sperm bank *for her* (*Marie Claire*).

Finally, a leering pansexual ocelot of a Scotsman came and drove us to the estate, where we met the trip's other riders: a moody Dutch princess of questionable historic lineage, a German architect (and Claus von Bulow/Willy Loman hybrid), and three small reporters from the BBC.

The duchess entered, and she was exactly as we'd imagined —lovely, genteel, and terrifying all at once. The kind of woman who was as at home elegantly apportioning tea to foreign dignitaries as she was cleaving a rattlesnake to bits with a machete. I'd had enough gin at this point to smile magnanimously and radiate a completely false humility, when the dining room door swung open, revealing the duchess's son Simon, who would be our guide.

I looked at him, and suddenly everything changed.

Simon. Simon Fontaine-Maddox. The oldest son. The firstborn. The man who would be leading us all. The man who, I knew in an instant, could command me to jitterbug in a flesh-colored unitard and I would obey. Simon produced several topographical maps of what was about to become my home and kingdom and asked if I wouldn't mind carrying the maps in my saddlebags. "Of course not," I said, knowing that soon I'd be carrying more than his maps. Simon. Dreamy, rugged Simon. He was stocky, and capably thick, with pink English skin and terminally blue eyes. The kind of eyes that, I was sure, were the pure genetic offspring of those cerulean blue orbs that had once surveyed, pillaged, and colonized countless unsuspecting nations and peoples. His hands were gnarled and dirty, hands that had tethered, filleted, and sheared any number of wild things. He wore one of those leather knife thingies that always look really queer on production assistants and TV home-improvement-show hosts, and I quickly fantasized that he'd probably set many a Highland lamb free from a nasty wire fence with this essential lifesaving tool. And whenever Simon spoke he would always finish by looking down and then directly up and at you—and you just knew that at that moment God was saying, "Okay, let's bring it in for a tight shot here."

The first three days of the ride were beautiful, and completely uneventful. The terrain was spectacular, but in that way that proves you're way too shallow to appreciate any kind of real beauty unless it's promoting Absolut vodka or you get it in a gift bag at the end of a chichi party. We galloped over fences and I horrified Trevor by wearing my Walkman because I was sure that Bono and Simple Minds were better purveyors of things Celtic than anybody else. Nor had we seen even one of the deadly peat bogs that had killed two riders the year prior.

I spoke to Simon often. He told me about his childhood, his Scottish upbringing, and the trauma that was English boarding school, where all he wanted was to be outside with the horses. I confided in him—completely falsely—that I had been equally miserable at American boarding school because I, too, longed to be with the horses. He nodded knowingly. And it was that forever-and-a-diamond kind of knowing. I tried to determine whether his glances my way could have been classified as burning, and decided that they could. He spoke constantly about his horse, Beatrice, and their symbiotic relationship, and when he stood next to her he would murmur into her ears in a vaguely sexual way.

He was the answer to prayers I didn't even know I'd had.

Suddenly, everything seemed as clear and as palpable as the astonishing purple moors that sprawled out ahead of me. I beheld vistas that were crisp, clean, and decisive. This place was exactly where I wanted to be. It wasn't just the freedom of the wilderness—I certainly didn't care about that—but rather it was the fact that I felt free from thoughts, constraints, boys, and direct mail. Or American Boys at least.

We rode seventy-five miles a day, stopping in the evenings at remote B&Bs where Simon taught me gently about all the beers I announced I was dying to try. So what if beer had been repellent to me for thirty years? It was now nectar and then some. Plus, Simon encouraged my intake of just about every digestive component of an animal's stomach the British eat, including items that looked like emergency-room drive-by-shooting specimens. Not to worry, though; I was hooked. If Simon wanted me to sample entrails, I would. I just couldn't believe it was happening this way, to me. I, a *drink-Coke-play-again* kind of girl, had finally found the most indescribable love of all. And here he was, seated next to me, contentedly swallowing some hapless pig's lower GI tract.

By this time Trevor asked if maybe I was going a little

overboard with my crush, mooning over this poseur hay-seed. *But he's so rugged,* I said. *He doesn't bathe,* Trevor said. When I snapped that Rob Roy probably hadn't either, he just stared at me and murmured that maybe there was a little Michael Flatley in all of us. Still, I knew that I was where I belonged—and that I was never, ever, coming home.

On day three we climbed a mountain called the Devil's Staircase, and as we began to gallop en masse across a dark, lush moor I knew I was the happiest girl on earth. It was then that I noticed the color of the grass begin to change dramatically ahead of us, which meant that we were entering one of the peat bogs. Suddenly I heard a shout, then a scream, and three of the horses ahead of me lurched and stumbled. Each animal seized up and sank eerily into the ground, making loud keening noises that were soon echoed by the screams of their riders. Arms, legs, feet, hooves, and tack spun into the air. I watched in still horror the late-twentieth-century Kenneth Branagh movie this had become.

The entire event took less than two minutes. When it was over, one BBC reporter had cracked two ribs, the German's perfect Aryan nose had been smashed to bits, and the tiny lesbian's wrist was sprained perpendicular. Curiously, I remained unharmed. Then Simon explained, somewhat ominously, that no matter how competent you are, a peat bog will snap a horse's legs in half in seconds. Of course, once you've seen fifteen hundred pounds of horseflesh sink three feet toward the earth's core, nothing seems really permanent.

Over lunch, between licks of Nutella smeared across hunks of good white bread, Simon comforted each of us. *Remember, the horse is your friend,* he said; *you must be kind to it—then it would perform, just like Beatrice, his trusty mare, always had.* I sat terrified, contemplating the precarious relationship between wheat and chaff in moments like these. After lunch we rode back down the Devil's Staircase, at a fifty-degree angle. I wanted to spit up at about five-minute intervals. Simon rode along beside me and complimented me on my sturdy tenacity, and I blushed and asked him how he could be so calm.

"I've got Beatrice here," he said; "there's nothing like this relationship." He stroked her lovingly, as he would me someday. And while I was mentally selecting bridesmaids, suddenly my horse plunged sickeningly forward down into a ditch, and I was thrown across his head deep into the ditch's interior. I could hear the earth—or another falling animal—rumbling nearby. And as the peat showered down and covered my face I heard Simon say, "Don't move," and I was conscious of staring skyward as an enormous animal came down toward me, only to bounce away before crushing me altogether. I blacked out. At the moment I came to, the only image that formed in my mind was a single cracked-pepper turkey sandwich at the Rockefeller Center Au Bon Pain. Then I blacked out again. When I finally awoke, my horse was standing blessedly unharmed, staring at me, looking relieved.

That evening everybody drank until we lost peripheral vision. It was that weird peril-based camaraderie where everyone feels relieved and jumpy at once. The one thing we all agreed on was that Simon had kept us all going, that if it had not been for him and his beloved Beatrice, we wouldn't be alive.

The next day's ride was equally terrifying, but we'd all had sherry shots and were slightly inured to it and we feigned a kind of bravado. Sure, people were injured. Bones were broken. But in a good way. This was what life was all about, what I was meant to embrace. And as we galloped across a lush expanse of what was to become my very essence, I happily considered the *new me*. Midthought, I watched as Simon's horse's legs buckled backward and she collapsed in a peat bog, making a terrible, sickening, crunching noise. He somersaulted over Beatrice and lay still, as she flailed in the mud, making a high-pitched noise I will never, ever, forget. My heart stopped. A mini-eternity went by. Then, like Lazarus, he slowly got up and approached her. "Get up, you motherfucker!" he yelled. "YOU FUCKIN' BITCH NAG! You shaggy-assed gluebound cunt!" And he began to strike her viciously with his whip until she scrambled to her feet and stood, dripping in sweat and shaking.

He looked up and smiled at all of us, but for me, it was too late. Game over. I could only gasp and stare, shattered forever by this maniacal display. Simon knew it too, for he quickly patted the terrified animal and cooed softly into her abused ear. "Right, then," he said softly to us all, "we're off." He cleared his throat, adjusted his cap, and we moved off slowly. The event was never mentioned.

The next two days, largely because of safe terrain, were

spent galloping across mossy moors and along the sea, which was fine. Whatever. I suddenly took to speaking to the other Americans—with whom I ended up having a lovely time. And more than anything else, I wanted to come home. Never again would I succumb to anyone's opaquely rustic persona. Never again would I fail to appreciate the innate and safe, healthy charm of East Fifty-fourth Street. And never again would I moon over Simon Fontaine-Whatever, baronial heir to unforgettable savagery.

the countdown

• • •

My brother Eliot's best friend, Eddie Meyerson, was the single object of my unrelenting affection for about the first twelve years of my life. Even though he had referred to me, by turns, as a creepy little ape, a jelly-mongering ferret, a cross-eyed rodent, and an itch. But the mere fact that he imbued these monikers with such creativity, that he took the time to describe (and therefore notice) me at all, made me swell with sticky adolescent love like some moony-eyed tick.

I compounded my own palsied approach to him by refusing to use his given name during my childhood, referring to him only as Sweet Love, Tasty Honey Boy, Mr. Fluff-BunnyFun, and a host of other terms that might now legitimately be confused with prison slang.

No one had heard from Eddie Meyerson in years, and of course it'd been eons since all of us kids had moved away from Philadelphia. But curiously, he resurfaced not long ago when I headed upstate for the self-flagellation, gnashing of teeth, and beating of breasts otherwise known as a ten-day family gathering. Mother has a cottage next to my sister's house in Nowheresville, New York, way west of the Hudson River, the route to which feels quaint as you speed through towns like Fish's Eddy but then feels creepy when you spot your fifteenth man climbing into a pickup with a hemorrhaging doe draped across his shoulders.

My sister Meg lives with her French husband and their daughters on the edge of civilization and a Finger Lake. It's all very bucolic, with lots of children and farm animals, virtually interchangeable, none of whom bathe, all of whom wander around in various stages of nudity. The kids have never had a Coke in their lives. They drink some kind of seltzer-based nectar and spend lots of time nibbling on fibrous pellets my sister buys in bulk at some Stalinist food cooperative she swears by.

Meg can do about a jillion and one attractive things with a pinecone. She is nearly six feet of holistic, ayurvedic, eye-of-newtic blondness, and I have lived for her approval since before I could spell my own name. So charismatic is Megan that, years ago, when she unwittingly attended an N.A. meeting, believing it to be Narcissists Anonymous, she was actually welcomed with open, if track-marked, arms. That's how charismatic.

Meg's six-foot-six-inch husband, Philippe, typifies a certain Gallic arrogance. He has that Catholic edginess that comes from years of wonder, which turns to skepticism, to fury, to numb denial, and then into the curled lip of disinterest. Mother has always been an enormous irritant

to Philippe. I think she typified for him all that is uncen-
sored, irrational, and controlling about American women.
Mother, on the other hand, is forever pointing out just how
very proud she is of *him.* She is constantly defending him. I
would ask her if this was because he was French, because he
was large, or because he had sired her grandspawn. Once,
she admitted candidly that it was sort of a combination of
the three. Personally, I find my brother-in-law difficult at
best, but when with him I also take pains to pepper my language with as many "*c'est-ças*" and "*bien surs*" as possible,
largely because he's the only person in Upstate New York
who can fix the alternator on my car. I have to give him
credit for being able to hold his own in our family, which is
neither easy nor typically too much fun. Megan has always
said it's just a good thing none of us have witnessed her
husband's hair-trigger temper, although I have no idea
what that means. I've always thought a hair trigger was the
thing that drug-addled GI snipers look through before they
blow off the skull of an old Vietnamese woman doing laundry in a river. But maybe not. Philippe is always careful
around me, too, because he knows that I am the volatile
child. In fact whenever there are Christmas parties upstate
and I have to meet their crunchy friends I am always introduced as *Elizabeth, who can be difficult.*

So this trip, I had not been in Megan's home for an hour
before I realized that our mother had cooked up a rather
elaborate plan. A last-ditch effort to prevent my eternal
spinsterhood.

"We have a marvelous surprise guest this week, Miss Pink," Mother said, descending the staircase and handing me a sheaf of clippings, as she did every time I saw her.

"Who?"

"Eddie Meyerson. Remember Eddie Meyerson?" She smiled.

"Eliot's Eddie? Yeah. And?"

"He's going to come stay," she said. "And he's looking forward to seeing *you*."

"Neat," I said.

"And now he also seems to be *divorced*," said Mom. "That nice Slater girl he married turned out to be one bad apple."

"That's unfortunate," I said, and tried to remember what That Nice Slater Girl looked like. And what she'd done to become so pommified.

"He's coming up Saturday. How nice will that be?"

"Pretty nice, Mom," I answered, as the hazy picture of what she was doing came into stark focus.

"So we'll all want to look after him. A little TLC never hurt anyone." Now I got it. Every planned, scheming, brilliantly orchestrated bit of it.

Of late, whenever the Nowheresville neighbors had wandered over for a drink or fourteen, posing the usual inquiries about everyone's health and marital status, I had taken to watching my mother like a hawk. Waiting for her to nod in my direction and quietly intone phrases like "we're optimistic" and "someday, but not yet" and the ultimate death knell—"career girl." Mother always believed that without spouse and spawn, one might as well be pushing up daisies.

Which is precisely why when Mother had learned via some Underground Protestant Gossip Railroad that our very own Eddie Meyerson had recently been divorced and was now living in New Jersey, she sprang up on behalf of her last cub. And her plan would go into effect this Labor Day weekend.

"Why are you so obsessed with this?" I asked her. "Do you know any other parents who do stuff like this, Mom?"

"Plenty. And why not? I want you to be happy. And if I can help, would it be so very tragic if—if you met some nice boys?"

"Because I live with rats in a sewer?"

"Because you haven't met any really nice ones yet. And because that's what mothers do. If you're going to go out there and declare you're a *career girl,* then you've already put yourself at a disadvantage. That doesn't mix well with a lot of men," she said, then added, "Men don't always think it's so *neat* to have all that one-upping going on." Just then Eliot walked into the room. He stared at her.

"What did you just say?" he asked.

"She's hell-bent to maintain a career, and that, I think, is sometimes *at odds* with what men want," said Mom.

"Mom," Eliot explained, "turns out, it's a fact of this era. That's not an option. She's working, she's good at it. And she's doing what she has to do to survive!" She glared at him. I was grateful, although both of them seemed now completely oblivious to the fact that I was actually in the room.

"You know, Eliot, *you're* not exactly creating a home for anyone—"

"Mom, that's bullshit!" Eliot yelled.

"Don't use that language with me," she said icily. Eliot rolled his eyes and walked away.

"I think he's tired," said Mom.

"Look, I think the guy thing will sort itself out," I said evenly. "I just wonder why you are so forcefully trying to engineer things. I'm going to be fine." Although I was not at all sure that I was.

"Of course you are, dearie," Mom said. "Now help me fold these sheets." She handed me a basket of fresh laundry.

Throughout childhood Eddie Meyerson had been a genuine cult hero. Mother had adored him and was forever suggesting to the members of her own brood that we either emulate or marry him. Bright, athletic, and clean, he'd been one of those folk figures who'd always pretty much excelled at excellence. Son of an egregiously prominent family, Eddie was polite, he was cute-looking, he'd been processed and trained at all the right schools, he stood up when a woman entered the room even during that three-year period in the late seventies when nobody else did, he remembered to call my dad Doctor instead of Mister. He helped clear.

Mother used to say, "Eddie's not the kind of fella you want to bring home—he's the kind of fella you want living there to begin with!"

Four days prior to Eddie's scheduled arrival, a curious sea change took over our little nondescript lake house.

Overnight, a family that had, for centuries, been perfectly content to spend an entire week sleeping, eating, arguing, and eating just a little bit more suddenly became whirling dervishes of cultural activity. Because Eddie was coming to visit—and I guess because my own future and dowry hung in the balance—we had to be active, interesting, and involved. This fix-up (which initially repelled me, then intrigued me, all the while rendering me inept with terror) prompted a maelstrom of athleticism and scholarship never before witnessed. Mother marched downstairs with *The New York Times Book Review* and announced that she was off to Barnes & Noble to purchase nonfiction. My sister went to buy flowers, even though the greenery in this spectacular and bucolic setting had long been sufficient. Philippe was asked to fix up the sailboat, which had lain broken and un-used since the Reagan administration, as we were going for a midnight sail if it killed us. There was touch football.

Eliot was dispatched to purchase several local papers, and within a few hours we were all experts on the many cultural happenings in every single flyspeckish hamlet dotting the Finger Lakes region. We were alert, unified, and mobilized. Our first endeavor was the theater. The following evening off we went to see Sam Shepard's *Buried Child.*

"You know, if it's any good, we'll bring Eddie back on Saturday night," Mother said.

Unfortunately, she despised the entire drama from the get-go, wincing at every outburst of subverted blue-collar rage. As we left the theater she immediately inquired just why American playwrights needed to glorify the despon-dency and wayward also-rans that seemed to litter Middle America. We all just rolled our eyes. Then she wanted to know if that *Sam Shepard wasn't that same one who was so busy shacking up with Jessica Lange, and if the two of them were so damn keen on each other, why the hell didn't they see fit to make it legal?*

So that wasn't an enormous success. So we'd try again. Within twenty-four hours we were seated sixth row orchestra— for the Syracuse Stage's production of Edward Albee's *A Delicate Balance.* Mother absolutely loved it. Eddie would too, she announced. We'd take him Saturday. She wondered why theater couldn't *always* be that way, unlike that ghastly *Buried Child.* Although she also took pains to point out that the two plots were, in her mind, essentially the same, only *Delicate Balance* had a much more attractive cast. And a considerably more appealing set. *You know,* she added, *Albee did go to Choate, after all—just like your father. And your brother. And Eddie Meyerson.* The fact that *I* had also attended—and been expelled from—said prestigious institution hung in the air like discount perfume. Then, to stir things up, I pointed out helpfully that Edward Albee is also, you know, *gay.* Mom looked surprised.

"He is?" she asked.

"As a four-day weekend," I'd answered plainly, happy to alter any preppy value-oriented notions she might have about Edward Albee. The subject was dropped immediately.

Even the food changed. What would once have been a simple calculation of forty or fifty wings for Shake 'n Bake now became the time and temperature required to purée and bake some complicated vegetable none of us had ever eaten in our lives. Silverware purchased just before the Crimean War appeared. A plan was carefully formed for a Friday night cocktail party, in honor of His arrival. But

instead of our usual Drinkie Bird neighbors, Mother announced that the Wallachs (he a tenured Classics professor
at the university in town and she a world-renowned author
of several books on Sanskrit texts) would be joining us.
Which prompted my niece to blurt: "But the Wallachs are
totally boring, and we have to lock all the animals up." Eliot
looked puzzled, and I explained that the Wallachs had severe
pet allergies—and that the reason for our animals' quaran-
tine was *not* because the couple was boring.

In the course of three days essentially we'd gone from a
typical and egregiously uninspired American family to one
that was interesting, committed, and pathologically engaged. I began to feel nervous; my sister's eyebrows would
lever up like a drawbridge whenever I swallowed anything
that even hinted at carbohydrate content. I was subjected to
a process of ablution with any number of Clinique unguents
and other items designed to make me vaguely desirable. I
was presented with top-of-the-line face creams and extreme
hair product. I was being groomed, actually fussed over, like
some vestal virgin awaiting a ritualized ceremony. It was a
little surreal.

All I could think of was why on earth would I be considered attractive to a shell-shocked divorcé? Then I remembered my job. My copywriting. My skill. My astonishing way
with the Hook, Line, and Sinker of Sell. That was something. For hours at a time there were headlines buzzing
through my head, kind of like the digital LCD news crawls
that streamed across Times Square buildings.

Even the grandchildren were prepped. I don't think they

were fully aware of the massive strategic campaign launched on my behalf. And quite frankly, it seemed unlikely that Eddie would find any girl whom he'd once seen deliberately swallow several locks of her own hair even remotely attractive. But by golly, I was going to try. In fact, I began to feel a little giddy. My awkwardly inert, passive behavior quietly took on a little purpose. Suddenly anything seemed possible. I was going to be lighthearted, damnit.

At 1 P.M. I sat quietly in a chair, grappling with the concept of "breeziness," and finally winning. I did have good things going on. At two-thirty my nieces and I reclined happily until it became clear that a trip to Wendy's was needed since He wouldn't arrive for another two hours or so. I obliged happily. The kids were thrilled and off we went. Slowly pulling through the drive-thru I smiled carefully at the gold band on our cashier's finger. That's nice for her. See? Somebody loves her, and, well, you just never knew when that kind of thing would happen. Who knew there could be this much promise in Nowheresville? Who knew life could ever be this accidentally rich?

Eddie Meyerson never showed up. We received a polite phone call explaining that he'd been called overseas to remedy a brewing pork-belly crisis on the Japanese stock exchange. He was terribly sorry. Within minutes the vegetable purée was tossed, and Mother was left to wade through the opaque tedium of conversation with the Wallachs. The grandchildren disappeared to some remote shed, where I'm pretty sure they had cigarettes hidden. My brother gently squeezed ketchup across a microwaved bowl of penne.

I stood on the dock overlooking the lake and tried to stand up straight. Tried not to hunch like some tragic figure who had voluntarily elected to stand alone on a dock at dusk in the first place, further illuminated by my own what-do-we-do-with-her-nowdom.

But the next day as I drove over the George Washington Bridge into Manhattan I was profoundly aware that for four brief shining days the golden light of something intangible, possibly creepy, but basically noble had shone upon us all.

yearning one's keep

. . .

It was just a class. And it meant nothing, really. There wasn't a lot of soul searching or forethought. Not even a lot of planning. It was just something I was curious about—even though my peers would, of course, construe it as gooey, earnest, and foolish. The kind of undertaking likely to prompt snorts of disgust from everyone I knew (including me). Because that's what we do when a person embarks on something as guileless and yearning-based as an acting class.

I don't really think men have a strong capacity to *yearn* like women do. Rare is the novel I have read (actually, that's a true statement in and of itself), but to continue, rare is the novel I have read where a man is described as *yearning* for something. This harks back to childhood. Girls yearn for breasts, acceptance, and riding lessons. Boys want to play hockey, harass insects, or attend baseball games, and when they don't get those opportunities, they sulk or get moody. But I really don't think they *yearn* so much.

Which brings me to actors. It seems that whenever a major leading man is profiled, a genuine movie star, nine times out of ten he'll claim his success is the result of an "accident." He got into acting because of an injury, or because his best friend was into it, and decent upstanding wingman that this guy was, he followed suit. Sometimes it happened because there was a pretty girl involved in the school play, so he decided to get involved in the hopes of a deeper personal involvement. Or maybe the Oscar he won started with something as simple as Shop wasn't available fifth period, but Acting 101 was. It always seems a profession that men fall into unwittingly. Or so their mothers or their publicists might like us to think. However, when you read about an actress who has achieved monumental success it is typically because she really, really wanted it—she yearned for it and it all started somewhere between the riding lessons and the breasts. She knew it *knew it knew it,* and it all began one day when she was probably five, when somebody had taken her to see *A Midsummer Night's Dream.* And that was all it took. So she worked and she strove and she hoped and she dreamed and she yearned. I myself had of course wanted to be an actress but during my senior year of college thought better of it. It was not going to happen. Which was disappointing.

Until I realized that *writing copy* could equal a vicarious life in the theater.

Writing copy is the perfect answer; it solves all the problems and fulfills the same creative goals; it's essentially a parallel world of performance. Because when you're writing persuasive copy, you require and legitimately employ all elements of theater. You have an audience that is (hopefully) rapt. You have a message. You have language with which to convey that message. And your job is simply to transform people with that message. Which is precisely why copywriters can actually lead wholly rewarding (and frequently better-paying) vicarious lives in the theater. Without the greasepaint, the heartache, or the trust falls. And so long as I was writing copy that elicited a visceral response from an audience, I would thrive.

Nor will I stop writing it. Despite the fact that I had officially resigned from Time, my structure-craving dark pumps (and landlord) were all too happy with my frequent trips back to Rockefeller Center for freelance work. And so was Sid Glassman, the grumpy journalist with whom I had managed to fall hopelessly in love. A man with chronic heartburn and a serious Alan Arkin complex, who was also patently unable to commit to anything more than a particular cable channel.

Sid was probably the funniest, smartest man I'd ever met. He was certainly the funniest, smartest man I'd ever dated. The relationship was doomed from the get-go, but he was so verbally intoxicating—and so radically different from Clark R. M. Wheeler, M.D.—that I felt punch-drunk and grateful even during his reprimands. He was shabby and learned, with glasses that spoke volumes (much like their owner). Eyes squinty from hostile intellectual debate. The hairline receding with a kind of talk-show dignity. And sneakers. Always, sneakers. Great, huge, twin-toned urban emblems of basketball prowess from Nike. Sid used to call them his Air Semites. Happiest upon a soapbox where he could empathically hold forth on West Bank politics, the Knicks, or Elie Wiesel, Sid felt if you had any smarts whatsoever, you should be effecting change or at least endorsing Ralph Nader. He embodied an arrogance-with-high-productivity-levels that I adored. And even though he had to remind me that he was a real writer and I merely an educated hack, there was something nice about simmering in the Crock-Pot of codependency. In fact, the sheer toxicity of it all armed me with a kind of abandon. It gave me the bravado needed to dip my toes back into the once-daunting tidal pool of theater.

The catalogue called it "Scene Study: Exploring the Language of European Playwrights." It looked perfect, largely because it met at night.

That was all. I hadn't mentioned it to anyone. But I had been thinking about the theater for a long time, and running into Walter Kimball had caused me to investigate further. Mother was delighted about my proposed venture. However, I also had to stress that it was a drama class I was taking—one that had nothing whatsoever to do with musical theater. Because right up there in her personal pantheon of success for me, just a few yards behind "Wife" and "Mother," one could find "Hoofer." And even though she recognized life in the theater as one of abject poverty and ridicule, she also, down deep, found it just a little bit glorious. More than once, I was certain, she'd secretly fantasized that I might get swept up by the magic of tap dancing and moonlight as a Rockette. Even with my good job, if someone noticed me shuffling off to Buffalo while pouring coffee at Schwab's Drugstore, all the better, as far as she was concerned.

But I was firm and clear that there would be no tap dancing. It was just an acting class with good old straight plays. "You know," I told her, "it's going to be serious dramatists. Like Chekhov."

"But Chekhov's so endless and bleak," she said. "And everyone dies wanting something ridiculous, like a plot of land or happiness or something."

"But that can be good, sometimes."

"Well, it's nowhere near as good as *42nd Street,* I'll tell you that much!" she said, reiterating her support and devotion to the musical that had been running on Broadway forever and that she had seen more than half a dozen times.

And in the years since I'd studied theater in college, apparently not much had changed. This was one of those ongoing classes, and clearly most of the students were returning and had been doing so forever. Each student seemed hell-bent on underscoring his uniqueness, and ultimately on securing the attention and approval of the teacher. Our acting teacher, one of the genre who may or may not have done a stint in *The Fantasticks* off-Broadway during a simpler time when he/she had more hair, plus probably several regional productions of *P.S. Your Cat Is Dead!* and maybe *The Effect of Gamma Rays on Man-in-the-Moon Marigolds,* before realizing that life is just easier and far more lucrative when you teach scene-study classes. So he/she can return to his/her spouse and chidren/animals in Nyack.

The class had twenty-four people in it. I was right in the middle, age-wise. There were young girls in halter tops and young guys who tried very hard to look dark and bruised. There was an older lady who ended all of her sentences in a singsong way, so we would all know that she'd done lots of musical theater. There were three men of average height and looks who I thought could work commercially, given their pleasant Everyman demeanor. It turned out that all three of them had. The class met weekly; it was three hours inside a black box on Forty-second Street. The first session was a breathing-and-get-to-know-everyone kind of thing, whereupon we were all assigned scene partners.

I was given a scene from a Noël Coward play to perform, and I wondered if this was because I happened to be wearing my skirt from work. Then the teacher handed out portions of scripts for the various scenes, and we all read through them. We were each given thirty-five minutes to do this, and I wondered why we needed quite so much time, since everyone appeared able to read. When the students returned and began to read their scenes, I suddenly noticed that regardless of whether the scene required it, every actor tried his or her damnedest to emit tears. Some exploded spontaneously, others sputtered and burst, and among some of the men there was a slow, bubbling buildup, like crude oil. This in turn made my delivery even more awkward and wooden, but because we were under bright lights and I was doing Noël Coward, I managed to inadvertently touch my audience as I (completely accidentally) came across as fragile and probably a little crazy. Largely because everyone else's crying was making me extremely uncomfortable. When it was my turn, the lights were so bright and my already ill-postured body so uncomfortably coiled that I could barely move. I do not think I had known a more arthritic moment. It became patently and hopelessly clear what a mistake this reinvestigation of the theater was. I wanted so desperately to be anywhere else that I spat out my lines scrambling across the stage like some twitching Tolkien corkscrew trying desperately to avoid knocking over furniture.

People came up to me afterward. It was bewildering.

"We could feel the implosion of your energy. How did you get your body to do that?"

"To deliver those lines like an injured, dying *animal*. What a character choice. Wow."

"*That's* commitment."

Dumbfounded, I squirmed out of that building like a common garden slug.

When I got home that night, I knew that no way was I ever, *ever,* going to try that again. Never again would I actively invite such humiliation, such withering embarrassment, such a reaffirmation of my already pronounced physical discomforts. No way would I subject myself to those teary slings and arrows. No way would I go back there to that touchy-feely environment that served, between the hours of 7 and 10 P.M., as everyone's personal Wailing Wall. Absolutely not.

Within a few years I would grow comfortable exiting Rockefeller Center in good shoes and silk dresses and traveling anonymously into a netherworld of dank spare-a-dime performance spaces and the narcissistic demons who breathe life into them. Most of my family would never know that the Little One was stumbling through evenings as a crack-addled prostitute, Julia Child, an overweight bumblebee, a menacing blind nun, or a leech-riddled Swedish Valkyrie Bride Creature Thing.

The trick to a double life, at least when you are kind of hapless, is remembering which people are part of which community. And while my two worlds rarely collided, one had to be careful. Not long after I reentered the theatrical atmosphere, I found myself starring weekly in a bizarre live late-night soap opera featuring drag queens and any number of outrageous off-color characters. Every Saturday night at 10 and 11:30 P.M., we spoofed the TV show *Dynasty,* and over the course of almost two years we gained a large and rather offbeat cult following. However, I never spoke about it to anyone who wasn't somehow connected to the show, and continued to feel that this compartmentalization was smart or at least adaptive. Sid paid little attention to it, as he was busy investigating Spanish Holocaust collaborators for *The Village Voice,* reading Philip Roth, and finding me high-maintenance.

Around this time I had started writing speeches for an

executive at an enormous U.S. oil company. He was pleased with them and especially liked one I authored for him to deliver in Tokyo. (The speech itself was cookie-cutter basic; all you need to do is mention *technical pathways toward global synergies,* and you're off and running.) His CEO liked it too, and soon summoned the author, who, he was sure, must certainly know something about Asia. Since I knew almost nothing about the region—the speech could just as easily have been given in Cleveland—this prompted a slightly awkward situation for me. Which became seriously alarming when, two months later, I was instructed to write a speech to be delivered by this same CEO to commemorate the official state transfer of Hong Kong.

This posed a massive problem indeed.

For not only was I unclear about who *owned* Hong Kong, I was also at a terrible loss as to where it was going.

"*China,* nimrod," Sid said, before adding that it was just a good thing I had nice legs.

And thus I spent the next seventy-two straight hours on the Internet and managed to cobble something together. If they had fired me instantly for my grievous ignorance, it would not have been in any way surprising. Curiously, they did not. And about a month later, when Hong Kong was restored to China, the oil concern invited me to a huge gala dinner at the Waldorf-Astoria. It was certainly flattering. But no way I was going to attend a corporate function where I might well be addressed by someone under the impression that I knew anything about Hong Kong other than what Worldbook.com had told me.

Things had begun to get rocky with Sid; harrowing and teary discussions could no longer be remedied by sex or a sporting event. He soon announced that any complaints I had about our relationship would need to be presented to him in writing for review. Possibly more preposterously, I agreed. Once he noticed the Waldorf invitation on the kitchen table, however, his tune changed. In that second my stock climbed, my legs grew shapelier, and I was placated with a box of Bugles and a back rub.

No way were we missing this. No fucking way were we missing Henry Kissinger, Maureen Dowd, Zbigniew Brzezinski, and free food.

An enormous fight ensued. Despite my protestations, however, Sid was determined. Which, in my weakened love-filled state, translated simply to *we were going.* It would be awful and mortifying, and my duped employers would be furious. There would be talk of global synergies and pan-Asian oil cartels, and I would never work for them again. Sid was thrilled to coach me, but even so, I remained heavy with dread.

When the evening rolled around, after the typical tears associated with begging one's journalist boyfriend not to wear "dark sneakers" with his tuxedo, we went.

There were three other couples at our table. They all knew one another, had exactly the same inflection, and could not have been less interested in pan-Asian petroleum relations. Or, for that matter, in us. Within minutes the evening morphed from a potentially embarrassing cross-examination into a disingenuous dinner with less-than-scintillating people and good cream-based chicken.

Everyone became seamlessly drunk. All three men were affably handsome, blessed with recent MBAs and nearly identical smiling, bony wives. Affably Handsome Man #1 told
me he managed the oil company's commodities portfolio. I
feigned comprehension and struggled to partition a flour-
encrusted dinner roll. Which is when I noticed Smiling
Bony Wife #2 staring at me from across the table. Caught,
she turned back to her husband and giggled. She did look
familiar, but in a generic way that left me puzzled. I'd attended (and been expelled from) any number of prep
schools and summer camps rife with lovely creatures like
this one. Her face wasn't ringing any bells, though. I racked
my brain and tried to put it out of my mind in that way one
does—thus sealing it permanently, a tiny and irritating
Post-it note on the inside of your eyelid. Sid patted my
lower back and whispered an entirely scathing critique of
the menu in my ear. When dessert was served, Smiling Bony
#2 again gazed at me for a long time before offering me a
cheery nod. I was irritated with myself because the cham-
pagne made me totally unable to place her. How did I know
this girl? Sid had managed to keep everyone laughing until
he brought up affirmative action, whereupon people began
to look nervous and Affably Handsomes #1 and #2 excused
themselves to smoke. When they returned, I caught both
Smiling Bony #2 *and* her husband stealing furtive glances
my way. Over port and coffee, the topic turned to Hong
Kong, wherein Sid revealed to the couple that I was the
CEO's speechwriter. At this revelation they stared at each
other and burst out laughing. I poked Sid in the ribs, be-

lieving that speechwriters should be anonymous. I was shocked by their outburst, however, and shrank into Sid's side.

"See?" Affably Handsome #2 crowed to his bride. "I told you!"

"Okay. You were right," she answered, patting him.

"*Now* you'll listen to me, right? I told you it wasn't the same one," he added, before turning to us and smiling.

"You'll have to forgive my wife. She thought she recognized you."

"Me?" I said. "Actually, I was wondering if maybe we went to school together."

"Um, no," Smiling Bony #2 interjected. "Not school. Actually, you're not who we thought you were. This is probably going to sound really weird, and we probably shouldn't admit this, but you remind us of this girl. This actress *downtown.* They do this like, crazy *soap opera* on Saturday nights. And you remind us of this girl in it. I mean not *exactly,* but—"

"What she means is you're much more, um, attractive," her husband chimed in. "The girl in the show is sort of a freak, but she's funny and we love going down there and it's this ridiculous little play thing—no one's ever heard of it."

"Really?" was all I could say.

"Yeah. You should check it out. It makes fun of *Dynasty,* and it's hilarious. And you just remind us of one of the characters. You sound like her and you look a little like her. It's weird."

"Hunh," said Sid. "How about that?"

"You look a lot like her, but you know, you're not. You're much better-looking, and you know, well, you're *here*."

Everyone laughed.

"Okay," I said. "Sounds like fun. Maybe we should check it out." I was grateful that for once Sid had kept his mouth shut.

Later, as I walked clutching his hand, I knew deep down that Sid probably wasn't going to last long. But he had kept my little embarrassing yearning thing quiet.

And that's how I got back into theater.

do they know it's halloween?

• • •

Children who grow up in suburban Philadelphia are rarely prepped for the day when they will be forced to break the law in order to avoid being fired from a job.

Nor had I ever imagined that eleven dollars an hour and reprieve from eviction would be worth risking imprisonment. Then again, I hadn't thought Radiohead, merlot, or Tibet would catch on in a big way either.

However, a few years ago, I was seriously in need of cash, having spent all of my earnings from a number of freelance corporate speechwriting gigs. (Having quit my full-time job, I was free to explore, and also free to contemplate my uneasy alliance with a regular revenue stream.) A friend of mine, aware of my disgust and deep-seated apprehension about Halloween, explained that he knew a way I could make some good money and get over various childhood anxieties all at once. A few drinks later, and after a terrifying look into the gaping maw that was November rent, I agreed to audition for Madison Scare Garden's Halloween

Show, the only job I could find whose sole criterion was my ability to show up. And in order to maintain my post as the Witch of Madison Scare Garden's Halloween Scream Park I would actively and illegally evade jury duty. And all it would take was a bottle of Wesson oil and two quarts of soy sauce.

When I was a child, Halloween was just a miserable failure of a holiday, since I lived in a neighborhood devoid of kids. Even when children did move in, the results were often disastrous. I remember when the Doughertys appeared in the big house next door, with three angelic girls of descending age and ascending cuteness. Thrilled by the prospect of children within my age cohort, I immediately marched over and welcomed the entire family. I was ecstatic with Moira, their youngest, who was exactly my age, eleven, and who was, she announced, really good at playing. However, the following week, when our elaborate plans for a tree-house razing were aborted by rain, we were confined to the kitchen, where tempers grew short. Disgusted by my malfunctioning Suzy Homemaker RediBake Oven, Moira got up, glared at me, and in guttural yelps revealed that her parents had warned her about me because I was a *rotten Prod.* And that everybody at Our Lord of Heavenly Rest School said that all Prods did was steal from everyone, blame the Catholics, and then turn *them* into maids and cooks. To this day I am stumped by this ecclesiastical delineation, although at the time all I understood was that I was evil and, as far as Moira Dougherty was concerned, not appropriate companionship. She stormed out of my kitchen, never to return or speak to me thereafter. There went the one other kid on my street.

The other hitch about Halloween in our neighborhood was that we lived next door to an enormous convent, where each year one really was required to perform extensive (and occasionally dangerous) tricks for two dozen nuns before being awarded anything at all. Nor was this limited to a simple somersault. Oh, no. One frequently had to execute an entire gymnastics routine, or compose and read aloud never-ending librettos. In addition to taking away valuable Treat-Gathering Time elsewhere, this was exhausting and—many of us felt—just plain wrong. Fortunately, I was double-jointed in my shoulders and could bring my hands back and forth over my head, which startled and pleased all the sisters. Although some of the nuns looked at me in that way that one might regard the Shroud of Turin, or something vaguely satanic that they ought to notify the Monsignor about.

My failed Halloween forays did change, however, when I met Loretta Scharparelli. Four years older, she simultaneously intrigued, repelled, consumed, and frightened me.

Loretta was terminally cool in that older, teenaged, breathless kind of way. And anyone who was fifteen and tolerated you when you were eleven—indeed engaged in conversation with you—was a friend indeed. She didn't seem to mind the pink tortoiseshell glasses with the one lens covered in sticky black masking tape to correct my wandering eye. She didn't mind that I could almost scratch my neck with my projectile front teeth. She didn't mind that one of my ankles was essentially perpendicular to my knee. Nor was she sickened by the two-inch lift on the sole of my hapless red oxfords. And sure, she wore clogs on Fridays in school with cutoff jeans shorts, which my mother considered trampy. And sure, she dated a guy who rode a motorcycle, which my mother considered trampy and criminal. But she was cool. And the Halloween after my eleventh birthday, she asked if I'd like to come trick-or-treating with her and some of her friends. This was a terribly exciting proposition for me, living in the Anne Frank Annex as I did, and I was delighted. To their credit, my parents, realizing that a Halloween spent with nuns was no Halloween at all, reluctantly agreed and dropped me off at the Scharparellis'. Theirs was a rather incongruous-looking Tudor-inspired ranch house, and it had been ghoulishly decorated to within an inch of its life.

Loretta immediately gave me a tour of the house, which was truly magnificent in its kitsch and Halloween spirit, something ours was definitely not. When we entered the kitchen, I asked why there were four mailboxes, one intact street lamp, and seven hubcaps strewn across the floor. "Oh, those," Loretta said. "Those are from last night . . . you know, it's all about mischief." Okay.

During the course of my tour I was plied with candy and told that it was going to be a long night. One by one Loretta's other friends arrived, each one at least fifteen years old, each one stunned to see me in my papier-mâché penguin costume. I could hear them talking over my head, saying things like "What's she doing here?" answered by "Legitimacy, man." Somebody else said, "Oh, I get it." Next thing I knew, the stereo was playing at full force and there was a mass exodus to the basement. I was invited down to see the "haunted house," which consisted of what I now know to have been at least four bongs, many boxes of Whip-Its, and several cases of beer and grain alcohol.

Loretta sat me down in the upstairs hallway and explained that my job was to be Penguin Mistress of the Crypt. Whenever little kids came to the door, I was to give them candy and send them on their way. But if big kids came, I was to come knock exactly six times on the basement door. Then, if Loretta approved them, I was to usher them downstairs. She explained that I could eat as much candy as I wanted and told me not to forget that I was the Most Important Person in this Haunted House.

At first I relished my role, escorting various ghouls downstairs and offering candy treats to dozens of children who came to the front door. After two hours I realized that we weren't going trick-or-treating. After four hours I realized that I had become very, very, very tired and felt quite sick from eating so much candy and inhaling so much smoke from the raucous party going on downstairs. I suppose I must have drifted off to sleep in the foyer, because the next thing I remembered was being carefully lifted into the back of a police car and ferried home to my horrified parents.

After that, I gave up on Halloween altogether and developed an adolescent antiholiday stance, which I may have to this day.

I managed to land the Madison Scare Garden Witch job from a field of thirty other actors. I sat nervously and scoliotically at the audition. To my left sat two impossibly handsome boys from Juilliard silently mouthing pieces from *Key Exchange* and either *Burn This* or *Blithe Spirit*—I wasn't sure which. To my right two elfin girls in baby-doll tees and jeans so petite they appeared to be conducting a rape in progress chattered happily and were hired as soon as each stood up. As I entered the audition room the casting director asked me simply to scream as maniacally as I could, and then to present proof of U.S. citizenship. Whereupon I was cast.

On the day I was hired, I received my second notice to serve on jury duty. At the time, I was still embroiled in an on-and-off romantic scenario with Sid Glassman, the bright, grumpy journalist. Sid told me to ignore the jury summons because now—finally—I was a working actor and that was the most important thing. Although he said in the end it wouldn't really matter, as all Protestants have a genetic predisposition toward that oblivious, proud decay and well-educated failure. But in the meantime, I should take this job and keep it at all costs.

At our first rehearsal, the seventy-five actors hired were shown around the vast expanse of the Garden. I quickly befriended an essentially topless dwarf who took me under her wing and explained that she worked in the straight white bonfire of commerce otherwise known as the Radio City Christmas Show every year—both in New York and regionally—and that she played elves and only elves, and that she would never be caught dead playing one of them *fuckin' faggotass panda bears.* I asked her if she had an extra cigarette, and she stared at me and said, *Well, they don't come twenty-one in a pack, but I'll give you one*—and I knew our bond was sealed. She told me that there was more money at the San Francisco Radio City show, but that the Boston cast had far better drugs.

There were seven attractions in the entire Scream Park, attended annually by some seventy thousand people. The producer took great pains to point out that we had been hired to scare the living daylights out of people, and so long as we showed up, we'd have job security for the run of the show. He was tireless and ultracharismatic, one of those people who really could inspire bitter, mismatched actors to freakish greatness daily. He also mentioned, repeatedly, that there was a great deal of security, if anything went wrong during the event. I thought this meant if patrons became too frightened and demanded an emergency exit or refund. However, my tiny friend explained that the security was, in fact, for us. Each year there were several casualties as a result of drunken patrons physically accosting and injuring actors. And every day money got stolen from the dressing rooms by—we could only guess—shifty wardrobe people on the lam. Or maybe by the security guards, who removed, it was estimated, more than thirty firearms from patrons of the Scream Park.

The show ran from three o'clock in the afternoon until two in the morning, and the clientele absolutely mirrored these hours. By ten-thirty there were no children, only cavorting teens, tipsy hoodlums, and silent, smirking people who had probably done time.

Within the first week three actors called in sick and were fired instantly. That same week I received my third jury summons and began to panic. I could not afford to lose this ridiculous job, but I desperately needed to get out of the other one. Which is why I finally decided to stop being such a wuss, behave like a grown-up, responsible witch, and figure out how to get fired from jury duty.

In addition to scaring the hell out of people, we were also instructed to vary our "scare styles" so as not to lose our voices or momentum. One learned to perfect the traditional "boo scare," then to add vibrato, quavering, and shriek oscillation to taste. Actors were stationed at one of the seven attractions, among them Dr. Shriek's House of Freaks, the Nightmare on Times Square Hotel, the House of the Seven Deadly Sins, and the Rikers Island Escaped Prisoners Maze.

Many of the actors played your garden-variety ghouls, or druid/zombie hybrids. Several carried torn and bloody appendages, many of which were accidentally left on the Craft Services table next to the bagels and potato chips, but you got sort of used to them.

A small, wiry man with gold teeth and crimson contact lenses wore only a loincloth and carried his two live Burmese pythons all the time. And, knowing a bit about constrictors in general, I was not surprised when at the Craft Services area the snakes (to which he was now oblivious) began to move about agitatedly as they became warmed by the many vats of soup and chili that were provided for the actors. This sent many other actors running in terror to the dressing rooms. In the House of Seven Deadly Sins, two women representing Lust wore only white terrycloth beach towels, the vast expanse of their exposed skin covered with bloody cornflakes to create the illusion of rotting flesh.

Everybody took their job very seriously, including two girls from Yale Drama School who explained quite earnestly to me that this was a job just like any other, and if you weren't prepared to *make choices,* you shouldn't be there in the first place. When I saw them standing solemnly in thirty-pound muslin druid robes in front of the 3-D House of Horror, I decided that they had made acting choices that hovered somewhere between postal clerk and museum guard.

The men in the Rikers Island exhibit, large, burly specimens who wore torn correctional-facility uniforms, appeared to have been airlifted directly from the pokey itself. Except for one inmate, a perky young song-and-dance man who'd recently completed a national tour of *Guys and Dolls.* By the second day, however, he was a snarling, vicious, incarcerated mess, entirely indistinguishable from the other actors. I wondered if the black man in cheetah loincloth and gazelle-bone beaded necklace who was called Jungle Boy felt in any way objectified, but then decided to keep that query to myself. The entire show had a not-even-subliminal component, and actors were hired with either personal freakish qualities or sexual desirability in mind. Two beautiful women wore striking white satin gowns and long kidskin gloves, and only when they turned around did one notice the filthy, blood-encrusted knives protruding from their backs.

As the sole witch in the Scream Park, I was posted in Scarewood Forest, which served as a haven for frightened children, a nursery, and a general area where I was instructed to roam and comfort children who were scared and scare children who looked comfortable. I basically ran the theme park's babysitting station, the one place where parents with older kids raring to go would leave their youngest and frequently weeping children to linger with me in relative safety. Some of the children colored; some wept.

Scarewood Forest was also the gateway where we ushered guests into one of the big attractions: the Occult Theater of Illusion, where two men in leather, one in an apron, the other in a wrestling singlet complete with a stainless steel codpiece, enacted a techno-Gothic magic show. Both had multiple body piercings, full-body tattoos, and hair in cornrows to their waists. Curiously, each of these Goth Warriors was soft-spoken and friendly in the Craft Services area, but once inside the theater, they became marauding, pillaging testaments to a kind of homoerotic occult magic show. My job was to usher 146 people into the theater every fourteen minutes. The show involved several writhing girls in bisque-colored unitards who were abducted by an enormous robot, only to be saved by one of the homoerotic Goth

Warrior Illusionists who plummeted down and swooped her up via a primitive zip line. During this time, the *other* Goth Warrior Illusionist played the synthesizer directly to stage left, until such time as he was needed for the show-down. At which point the music continued miraculously onward *without him.* Against a deafening techno beat, the girls were padlocked inside crates, but the locking and chaining procedure took so long to complete that specta-tors actually forgot they were hidden in the first place, thus diminishing the thrill when the girls emerged fifty feet away. The audience loved the show. Four times an hour, nine hours a night, these men were kings.

I was frequently reminded to frighten as many people as I could, which, given the amount of makeup, oozing sores, and latex on my face, was possible simply by asking an un-suspecting person the time. After two weeks, my situation reached a crisis point when my fourth notice to serve on jury duty arrived, with its accompanying threat of "punitive action or imprisonment" if I failed to comply, followed by a letter ordering me to the courthouse. I panicked at this rock and hard place of just getting by. I couldn't afford not to work. Which is when I decided that it's better to show up for an awful job that pays you than sit through an even more unpleasant one that didn't. So I devised a plan to take Sid's advice and get myself fired from jury duty.

Now, I'd been told early on that you could usually make outrageous claims that reflected bigotry or prejudice and thereby be deemed unfit for jury duty. I'd had friends who had simply and deliberately made horrifying remarks like

"Neither foreigners nor Canadians can be trusted" or "I don't have a problem unless it's with the Puerto Ricans—they're so shifty," or blurted out the ever-popular "Who says the Indians were here first? Look how much they drink!" Unfortunately, nowadays City Court magistrates knew every trick in the book. So I took a white T-shirt, tore it down the middle as violently as I could, and let it soak overnight in two quarts of soy sauce. Then I combed Wesson oil through my hair and parted it in the middle, and gave a seventh-grader in my building fifteen CDs in exchange for her aqua rectangular eyeglasses. Then I stepped on one of the lenses so it was completely shattered within the frame. I spent a dollar on a triple XXXL chartreuse down parka. And finally, I took one of my father's old prescription pads from the Institute of the Pennsylvania Hospital, the psychiatric hospital where he had worked until his death a few years prior, and wrote myself a daily prescription for five hundred milligrams of the antidepressant Paxil. Then I took the subway to the courthouse, having zipped up the green parka to my chin, trying not to asphyxiate myself with the smell of soy sauce.

At the courthouse, I told the magistrate I'd be more than delighted to serve on jury duty because I was fascinated with "the evil that men do." I also explained that it was frequently hard for me to focus emotionally. I underscored this visually by keeping my genuine wandering eye at a ninety-degree angle to my nose the entire time. The guy was clearly disturbed about the fact that he could focus only on one eye, and as he squirmed uncomfortably in his seat I noticed that he would shift his glance from one of my eyes to the other. He asked me questions, and I ended each of my answers with an unintelligible mumble. When he inquired, I'd say things like "Nobody understands, because Everybody Loves Raymond Burr . . ." before laughing as maniacally as I could. I punctuated my sentences with bad words and ran my fingers through my hair at forty-five-second intervals, before staring longingly at my greasy fingertips. He asked if I was warm in my down parka indoors and I replied that "it's always cold in New York, if you know what I mean . . . because it's all about the man."

When he asked what I did for a living, I replied, "Oh, *stuff*," before explaining that my lethargy was "probably due to some weird strain of Lyme disease because I'd been in contact with a lot of ticks last summer."

I explained that the doctors had given me these pills for my Lyme disease fatigue and then presented him with my prescription. He commented that the doctor had the same name as me; I told him I knew that, and that this was the only doctor I'd been able to find in America who wasn't part of those Pinko Stalinist HMOs that are ruining our land. I then asked him about *his* doctor, and *his* feelings about those Communist HMOs, and was told politely that he worked for the City of New York, so that wasn't really an appropriate topic. He closed my file and explained that perhaps I shouldn't serve on jury duty this time around, and that maybe I could come back once my Lyme disease cleared up.

I left the courthouse and raced into the subway, ignoring

the looks of commuters whose noses shriveled and twitched as I approached reeking of soy sauce. I raced to the Garden, sat for two hours in makeup, and went off to my job, which was—now that I'd been fired from jury duty—blessedly secure. And even though I still had that black heart and the empty life, I am not immune to the bounty of spectacle, and I actually grew to enjoy Madison Scare Garden. Throughout this entire show one grew to appreciate—and almost rely upon—the consistency of it all, always encountering the same set of reactions. There was the joy in seeing a child grapple with curiosity, then shriek, then laugh. Or the deeply personal horror I felt when a kid cried and begged to go home. Nor do you ever get inured to it: the screams that accompany the seventy-fifth overturned Coke are as poignant and resonant as the first.

So sure I'd broken the law, and sure I'd shirked a civic duty so that I could keep a post that served no good to mankind whatsoever.

But who wants to be one of twelve angry men when you can get paid to wear latex?

openly bicoastal

• • •

I arrived in Los Angeles with a dog, a cat, a laptop, a bathing suit, a genuinely false air of humility, and about fifteen magazines because a writer I knew told me that places can either have palm trees or literature—but never both. The date was July 16, during the twenty-four hours of which America experienced horrible tragedy. John Kennedy, Jr.'s plane went down. This was genuinely devastating. And if that wasn't enough legitimate misery, *Eyes Wide Shut* opened nationwide.

I had flown on Continental, seated next to a pathologically friendly man who wore a dust mask during the entire trip, rather like some kindly Hannibal Lecter, frightening me only when he warned me about the *nucular* and atmospheric dust that could get trapped in one's *lar-nyx* at thirty thousand feet.

"So. Um. Why ya moving to Los Angeles?" he'd asked cheerily as the Boeing 737 descended upon Southern California. And I remembered my brother had recently remarked that I wasn't so much a human as I was a metaphor. But that wasn't necessarily it, either.

So, I had just looked at the Man in the Iron Dust Mask and said: *"It's unclear."*

Which may be the most honest response I have ever given anyone on earth.

I arrived, and my friend Mary met me at the airport. She had already found me a cute apartment in the Prada garment that is West Hollywood. The building staff couldn't have been nicer, and there was a small Latin American rain forest in the lobby. The apartment was spotless and densely carpeted with great huge windowsills upon which my dog perched like a young cat.

Dr. Cogan had been pleased with my Year Abroad decision. We planned to have phone sessions. She had agreed that perhaps California might be a better place for someone who wrote, performed, and didn't mind driving. There was a certain *why not?* quality to it. She had, however, cautioned me to take it slow at first, specifically explaining that the first thing you do after you move to a new city is quite likely to shape your entire experience. Which I hadn't really understood initially, but which became clear when I set out to buy my first real household item. Which would be a major appliance. Apparently, the only hitch with my nifty little apartment, it turned out, was that the dishwasher was broken beyond repair and no one had had time to replace it before my arrival. The building manager explained that if I wouldn't mind going and getting one myself, I would be fully reimbursed. So off I went to buy said appliance. And this was exactly the first big project that Dr. Cogan had been talking about.

So it's Day One of my Year Abroad, and I'm all about completing this first big task. I spent a great deal of the morning fielding calls from relatives, their gentle tones suggesting that I had gone to California to recover from/ dry out from/find inner peace over something.

And that's when Mother phoned—for the third time in as many hours. She had given up on her dismay and was now attempting to help me get on with the brand-new life that I had so foolishly elected to try.

When I told her that I was off to buy a dishwasher, there was a very long pause on the line.

"A dishwasher? Lambchop, that's a mighty big step. Why don't you just get some T.P. and lightbulbs and call it a day?"

And all I could think was, *Nope. No way. This is my chance to shine. This is it. It's High Noon at the I'm OK—You're OK Corral.*

It's the Little One's chance to do something all by herself.

So it's Day One, and as I drive down La Cienega Boulevard I begin to feel the first ugly tinges of what would become full-blown car consciousness. I drive a 1994 teal green Ford Escort. An LX no less. In Manhattan, this is a perfectly legitimate vehicle. It's actually cool in an ironic, everycar way. Here, not so much. At an intersection I begin to notice the cars around me. There are tiny starlets in vehicles that could probably transfer Rhode Island to the West Coast if necessary. There are open Jeeps with seminude men obviously hell-bent on concealing their identities with baseball caps and dark glasses. There are Rolls-Royces con-

veying women with helmet hair to the Ivy. There are Range
Rovers for people who want to make a hell of a statement
really quietly. And there's me in my suddenly sophomoric teal
green Escort.

For dishwashers, a random survey directed me to the
barren outpost of civilization known as West L.A., to an
enormous, brand-new appliance store.

I marched up to a brightly colored information desk, behind which a bored actor sat thumbing through a Mamet
script. He was seated behind fourteen inches of thick bullet-
proof glass. I'm always made uncomfortable speaking
through those tiny speaking holes in the glass, even though
I am a paying customer and thus, theoretically, I am Queen
of the Transaction. Still, the hole makes me nervous and I
tend to stammer into it. I always hope they'll hear me, the
first time, and pray they won't make me shout out something back to them, like my IQ or bust size. He paid no attention to me, as I held no significance to him; he only
looked up when he'd memorized a significant portion of
American Buffalo. When I asked about dishwashers he looked
directly at my ring finger before pointing up some stairs.

On the second level I was immediately presented with a
dozen balloons and assaulted by several shrieking, extremely frightening clowns in whiteface and iridescent wigs
whose job, it seemed, was to direct me to the stereo department. Here, I was told, I would soon enter the "wicked phat
magical kingdom of monster woofers and ass-kicking cus-
tomized sound rigs that would blow my doors off and turn
my boyfriend on."

I explained that, despite what must be earth-shattering offers on bone-crunching sound apparatus, all I really wanted was, um, a dishwasher. The alpha clown standing next to me frowned, and I immediately felt guilty, even though his clown paycheck was unlikely to have been impacted either way.

Trying desperately to appear composed, I threaded my way through a Mojave Desert of television sets and noticed a group of large men in suits, with those telltale tiny microphones behind their ears. And, just like every other American who feels sneaky and wise for having recognized members of the Secret Service, I wondered who they were protecting.

I edged closer, careful not to attract the attention of the Secret Service guys or the Insane Clown Posse still lurking about. And I saw a small man watching a Sony Trinitron and realized it was none other than Kofi Annan, the Secretary-General of the United Nations. I stared at him, realizing sadly that this would hardly constitute any kind of important celebrity sighting to anyone I knew. The guy was a washout. For despite the fact that this man had probably stemmed the eruption of many potential wars, saving the lives of thousands of people in the process, his name never came up at our Game Nights, *Access Hollywood* had never done a field piece on him, nor had he been nominated for anything held at the Dorothy Chandler Pavilion.

Leaving the Secretary-General, who had, by this time, been undone by an apparently side-splitting floor-wax commercial, I went upstairs. Nothing was going to stop me from completing my mission. There, I was greeted by a leering jackalope of a man who smiled, welcomed me to Large Appliances, and asked if he could put value in my life. I explained that while I hoped so, what I really wanted was for him to put a reasonably priced dishwasher in my kitchen. He laughed lustily before escorting me down a corridor of refrigerators, any one of which could probably have given me crushed ice and jettisoned nuclear warheads simultaneously. He pulled me aside and asked conspiratorially if I'd seen the security guards downstairs. I nodded. Then he whispered, "See? Even Morgan Freeman needs appliances."

After a great deal of probing and cajoling on his part, and hearing about his time in the Mekong Delta looking for Charlie, I was the proud owner of the most spectacular dishwasher in North America, one with a rebate and a warranty that would extend well beyond my own death. It was an extraordinary feeling. My first task was completed. And as the men began to pack up the white machine for its delivery I just beheld its glint, marveled at its energy-saving features, and knew deep down in the tiny carbon chip that serves as my heart that this was indeed the most marvelously crafted, the most superb-looking dishwasher I'd ever seen.

I breathlessly bounded out of the store. I'd done it. All by myself. And the first thing I had to do was phone my Doubtie Doubterson family and tell them about the supremely grown-up mission I had accomplished. I didn't have a cell phone yet, but I spied a pay phone across Pico Boulevard. I happily jogged across the empty avenue, head held high, receipt in hand. It was going to be a good year.

And even as the officer slowly wrote up my first jaywalking citation, my spirits didn't flag. And the three parking tickets I amassed later that afternoon didn't dampen my resolve either. No, no. Nothing could stop me now. I was still elated at eight o'clock that evening when they discharged me from the Cedars-Sinai Emergency Room with seven stitches in my calf for the flesh wound I'd sustained from a hit-and-run cyclist. Nevertheless, I was still en fuego. *Nothing* would cloud my Day One euphoria. Even as I dragged my stinging, bandaged, blood-soaked leg onto the inflatable mattress that would have to do for the first few days, I felt like I was somebody. Which was a good thing, because you know you're *nobody* in West Hollywood if your dishes aren't clean.

with friends like you, who needs leprosy?

· · ·

Coming as I do from an enormous family where each member feels the need to describe childhood using overly dramatic language and Movie-of-the-Week motifs, and where many maintain a secret curiosity and adolescent envy of everyone else's looks, intellectual capacity, or net worth, I suppose I enjoyed a fairly normal upbringing.

And as is typical of such Americana, I grew to develop and cultivate a sort of cool indifference toward holidays. Thanksgiving I think made its way onto the calendar because it's pretty outside, with parents throwing a huge meal to divert their children from asking exactly why we'd bumped off all those Indians in the first place, if they were so important to our nation. Memorial Day and Labor Day seem to me little more than start and finish dates for all major construction roadwork on the Long Island Expressway. The Fourth of July is fortunate in simply being the final "Best if eaten by" date on all frozen hot dogs purchased in the winter. And as for New Year's, I continue to feel that anyone who uses phrases like "excited by" or "happily anticipating" or "can't wait for" in connection with this day is quite simply a liar or an infant. Then, of course, there's Christmas.

On that day in our family there's the standard excitement/anticipation of childhood, the furious need to blend of adolescence, the obnoxious, blasé ennui of the later teens, and finally, the somewhat resigned, introspective sentimentality of adulthood. Every year Mother reminds us that Christmas really *is* for the children, and every year I stop myself from inquiring, then, why the rest of us need to be a part of it at all.

Of course, it's that time of year when everyone walks around New York feeling irritated and wondering why all the tourists have to come and walk slowly in clumps around our city. And I often want to ask these people if they walk quite so slowly and clumsily in *their* cities, or if it's for our benefit. I find the holiday season a time of usurped cabs, blocked perfume counters, and screwed-up brunch reservations.

And Christmas is when I have to deal with my brother Malcolm.

My mother announces every December that the only thing in the whole world that she wants is for Malcolm and me to open up lines of communication. I should preface this by saying that my mother never says she wants anything for Christmas. Nor has her silence ever been a result of any altruism or selflessness. Rather, she has everything she could possibly ever need and want. Pretty much on earth.

But every year she proclaims that there are problems enough without her two youngest children barely speaking and all.

She also emphatically ties the decline of our nation to (1) various Democratic administrations, (2) those criminals writing filthy, murderous screenplays in Hollywood, and (3) that "single mother phenomenon everyone seems so crazy about."

Thus, to be crafty, every year Mom asks me to deliver Malcolm his Christmas presents. By hand. Thus forcing an encounter. Since he married Reidy, who is pregnant now, Malcolm has never come for Christmas. They always go to the in-laws in Darien. Sometimes both Malcolm and Reidy put the *arch* in *hierarchy*.

Malcolm's a pretty arrogant guy, the second-youngest to me by seven years, and he genuinely fancies himself an entrepreneur. I view him as impatient, stubborn, and distracted. He is, however, whoppingly successful, so my views don't count so much. We have never gotten along. He continues to treat me like I'm his scratty kid sister. In fact, the five older kids—who seem to get along with him just fine— say it's simply that he felt displaced when I came along. We speak once a year, and it's usually marked by a kind of highly combustible civility. He hates my artistic endeavors and side life in the theater. He told my mother that he thought it foolish—and a financial tragedy—that I'd thrown away a perfectly good college degree and quit a good job to pursue what he called a "fleeting Pinko career in the arts."

Thus, at Mom's urging Malcolm calls me to arrange our

Christmas Present Handoff Meeting. And just to be more of a jerk, he always calls around noon and asks if, what with my flaky lifestyle and all, *he's woken me.* Generally the event has been at a place of his choosing, like the Union League or the Racket Club or some other testament to scotch and Manifest Destiny. And there's a great deal of shoulder squeezing with all the other successful people there. Lots of "Malcolm, how marvelous to see you here" kind of thing. With "regards to the little lady"—and nobody's even looking at me. Usually I scowl and try very hard to look like his un-likely urchin sister or at least an unclean scullery maid. One year I blacked out my two front teeth when I had to go meet these members of the ruling class. Malcolm used to say, "Well, someday we'll have to meet some of *your* friends."

To anyone listening this would seem a perfectly natural remark. But I don't think he means it at all. I think he sees me as fair-to-middling with fair-to-middling friends. Which naturally prompts me to begin brooding upon all of this scorn. For days.

So this year, for the first time in many years, I've selected the meeting place. It's one of the cafés that my friends fre-quent. Yes, Malcolm. I have *friends.* This way he'll see that I'm not a complete misfit toy and I'll have the home-court advantage. The gift exchange will be swift and painless, as simple as a briefcase passed between spies in an airport.

See, when we were little I looked up to him like crazy. I had crushes on all his friends. I embarrassed him constantly and was always underfoot. He would talk to me or play with me when there was absolutely and entirely nothing else to do. He resented that the big kids placed him in a category with me, rather than with them. Then he developed a mean streak and became rather manipulative. Never a bully, he perfected a way to make me do things I'd invariably regret. Like one morning in January when I was six or so he woke me out of a sound sleep and said, "Quick, Rodent, it's Easter—let's go look for eggs!" So we both went outside. Sure enough, buried in a snowbank we discovered a brightly colored egg. "You're off and running now, kiddo," he'd said. I spent the entire day searching in the three feet of snow that covered our entire property for the other Easter eggs. By dusk, I had failed to locate another one.

A few years later, when Easter really did roll around, as a Sunday School assignment each of us was to stand up in front of the church and tell the entire congregation what Christ's Resurrection really meant to us. Malcolm sat me down the night before and told me exactly what to say, and just how to phrase it, so I could impress the whole congregation. The next morning I proudly declared the Gospel according to Malcolm. I announced that after the Crucifixion, Jesus ascended in one of those great big see-through elevators to a super deluxe Courtesy Lounge, where coffee, pastries, and use of the phone were complimentary. I explained to the four hundred horrified onlookers that Jesus remained in that Courtesy Lounge for three days (and that he also got to wear a monogrammed terrycloth robe) before being transported back to earth on the special Courtesy Shuttle.

So the annual handoff is afoot, and I'm seated in our

agreed-upon low-key café on December 20. And I'm snorkeling through the white fluff of a latte whose price tag would safely eradicate Third World debt. Inevitably it's one of those places with waitresses who wear perfectly clean white Gap V-neck T-shirts and lipstick we'll call *liver* and the ubiquitous clunky black shoes. And they invariably have a satin cord around their neck, from which dangles either (a) a hollow silver ball whose resonance can be picked up only by several sensitive dogs in the neighborhood, (b) a variation on the crucifix theme, indicating either a spiritual side or the deliberate condemnation of such, or (c) keys.

These are the same low-key café waitresses who roll their eyes skyward when you ask them to identify a certain pastry (in that *if you gotta ask* fashion—though they themselves were total neophytes two months prior). And as you watch one of these waitresses roll those eyeballs, you also know with certainty that despite this latter-day Diana Rigg's attitude this very second, she was also once the proud owner of a poster featuring a tiny kitten hanging perilously from a branch above a tagline that read "Hang in there, baby—Friday's comin'." And you just know that if you met her at a party and got to know her a bit, within seconds she'd bum a cigarette and say something complimentary about a piece of jewelry you had on before telling you that it reminds her of this really beautiful something she herself had treasured— and lost—that was a gift from her grandmother. Who, she'd say, was "really great," in that way that some people describe grandparents when they want to make them sound particularly modern or hip. As if to distinguish them from all the other retirement-home inmates who seem to have begotten everyone else's parents. And when she finally brings your latte, it spills and she giggles. The giggle that has exonerated her from blame for a million careless things she's done.

Then of course the stereo system plays Debussy, which can get irritating because he rambles so and never really goes anywhere. And you wonder if Debussy ever finished anything, ever. And of course you don't know the faintest thing about people like Debussy and maybe he was one of those guys who had consumption or some delirium-inducing illness, which is why his music never has any closure. And then you wonder what he'd think if he were to learn that his music would someday inspire light, tasteful banter in a cheery, warm café at Christmastime.

And here I am waiting and sipping. Pondering the home-equity loan I'll need should I desire maybe pie or carrot cake, or a slice of their special fresh banana walnut cumin fennel rhubarb bran muffin loaf. I decide against it. And I begin to chatter with the half dozen people I know at my table. These would be my friends. People I call pals, people to whom I would go with anything on my mind, people I have a vague sense of basic happiness among, but people whom I have never even thought to scrutinize. And as I address them I begin to feel defensive. About them. I wonder how somebody like Malcolm might assess them. And then I gently but firmly remind myself that I really don't care what Malcolm thinks. But at least he can get a look at them. These freaks. I know that's what he'll think. That's just the kind of thing he'd think. A couple are actors. One is a play-

wright. And one is an architect. In my mind I begin to mull
over the unsavory traits of each that are likely to pique my
brother's distaste.

On my left is Doug, an actor. Doug is straight, white,
earnest, appropriately liberal; his size allows him to wear
sleeveless flannel shirts and talk about a former life in rural
Ohio that he may or may not have lived. He has the kind of
forearms that look best crooked atop the door of a dark
green pickup, adjusting a rearview mirror before waving at
an intersection to the one girl who, years ago, just "needed
her space." Doug waits tables on West Broadway in one of
those places regulars call a bistro, critics call a hot new
eatery, gallery owners call home, and the rest of us call loud
and expensive. Doug has two cats, Gracie and Balloon. His
best friend is gay and has been hopelessly in love with him
since their sophomore year at NYU. Doug discovered the
Violent Femmes and falafel less than four years ago. And
despite his hectic schedule, he is free for lunch every single
day of the week. Doug's agent claims to be submitting him
on a daily basis, but two print ads for Stridex pads, an auto-
insurance spot, and starring roles in five student-thesis
films (each detailing an introverted young woman's coming of age in or around Central Park) are the extent of his
oeuvre. These forays, while providing endless fodder for
lamentation, aggravation, and a kind of charming despair,
have left him frustrated, to say the least. I have had a crush
on Doug since time immemorial, but when pressed he has
confessed that I'm one of those girls he finds slightly frightening. But in a good way, he assures me. And he says he's

always felt more comfortable with those girls from the student films, each of whom has left him longing and wondering privately if maybe he *shouldn't* have bought them jewelry at Pier 1.

Across the table is my friend Lila, an actress of absolutely indeterminate age, with hair one would simply refer to as "dark, with a history," minty white skin entirely devoid of pores, and lips permanently stained claret thanks to her MAC discount at Henri Bendel. Lila smokes all the time, drinks coffee, and subsists exclusively on poppy-seed bagels, romaine lettuce, and Jujubes (the latter causing her little finger to reside permanently in and around her upper-molar region). Nevertheless, people find Lila so charmingly waiflike, her gestures so lithe, that were she actually to ply a tooth loose from her jaw it would appear no less abrupt or shocking than if she had brushed lint off a sleeve. Conversationally, Lila is always engaging. She's one of those people who never initiate or open a discussion—she simply resumes where you and she left off earlier. The fact that the last conversation may have taken place eighteen months prior is unimportant to Lila. Every person she encounters is quickly recognized, and the last topic of discussion is conjured up, be it her grandmother's hip condition, her brother's pending record contract, her sister's rejection of the Forum in favor of "the Twelve Steps she's been avoiding all along," or her aunt's reluctant emergence from a none-too-surprised closet. And like a patient child who is finally shown to the box of Magic Markers at an adult party, Lila can always engage herself quietly. She is bright, articulate, enormously opinionated regardless of her own frame of reference or topical knowledge—and utterly devoid of humor. Which is not to say that she doesn't laugh. But she's one of those people who laugh convulsively at certain things and not at others, with no discernible cause or pattern. She also acts like she doesn't really care about fields like astrology or things homeopathic, but secretly I know she does. I know she spends money on candles.

Then there's my friend Ray, the architect. Who regards himself as considerably more easygoing than he actually is. And who hangs out with actors largely because he appreciates their collective despondence more than anything else. He appears at any and all theatrical events. Sober, he's innocently enthusiastic about his thespian colleagues. Drunk, he'll tell you that he's so over one-acts he could scream. He also told me once he'd rather have a knotted rope pulled through his lower intestine than sit through a staged reading of anything. Ray is thirty. He has very blond hair that struggles gamely to cover his skull, culminating in five or six errant wisps over his brow. He's got peridot eyes hooded by black hexagonal glasses we think he bought in Los Angeles. He wears only rayon shirts, each one bearing a small illustration or organism replicated a jillion times across the entire garment. In his spare time he arc-welds stainless steel engine parts and hopes someday to mount these installations in bank lobbies. Ray's girlfriend, Marika, is from Honduras. Personally I think he dates her because she offsets his own milquetoast sensibilities. I think she embodies that sense of "Other." She's in book publishing. She dislikes coffee and hates actors.

At the other end of the table, examining the seam of her floral print dress, is Rachel. She is now a playwright, who has weathered her own developmental storm and has a remarkable sense of humor about it. Rachel was my college roommate. I was with her on the day she kissed her overtly protective parents good-bye freshman year, and I was with her when she kissed a full scholarship to Michigan Law good-bye, deciding that she would never feel totally confident in a courtroom because there were too many variables to which she'd become emotionally attached. She told me she'd rather be in a profession where she could make damn sure of the outcome, and one could only do that, she'd reasoned, by authoring it herself. Her plays weren't bad, either. She'd gone through a sticky absurdist period, become obsessed with Molière for a summer, then written five abysmal one-acts about boorish men before settling upon postmodern drawing-room comedies, which she churns out with amazing regularity. Rachel is the assistant concierge at a hotel on Columbus Circle, and she gives any of us who want it *The New York Times* for free every day of the week.

I decide rather confidently after this inspection that despite whatever has been said by my brother, I have nonetheless managed to develop close personal relationships with people who are not entirely devoid of merit.

Suddenly in walks Malcolm. Once inside the door he

stops and stares. He squints because he thinks it makes him look more rugged. Which is actually true. He's terribly good-looking. For a fascist. He's got packages under his arm. And all I can think is no way did he wrap them himself. My friends all giggle because they've been hearing about Malcolm for years. I get up and walk over to him. I make contact.

"Hi, Mac," I say. "Happy Christmas."

"Hey you. Hello. Is this where you hang out?"

"When I'm not loitering or wantonly wasting America's tax dollars."

"Yes, of course," he says. "It's warm in here, though. Not so bad."

"How's Reidy?"

"She's good. She's due in three or four days."

"Tell her I say hi. And congratulations."

"I will. "

"Those are your friends?"

"Yeah." He scans them like an explorer gauging the Himalayas.

"They look nice enough."

"Well, they are, actually." Privately I feel a hot tear welling in my left eye.

"Hey, this is for Mom." He hands me a package.

"And this is for you guys," I say as we execute the gift transfer.

"Good to meet you, man, we've heard a lot about you." Doug pleasantly offers my brother a beefy hand.

"Hi. Me too."

"How about a cup of coffee—do you want to sit down? Is somebody helping you?" Diana Rigg has made a beeline to our table. She pulls out a chair.

"Yeah, Mac, do you want to sit?"

"Oh, thanks. Listen, I'd love to stay but—"

"I know, Mac. Happy Christmas."

There's a gratuitous peck on the cheek, and he's gone. The entire transaction took less than three minutes. Despite our shared DNA relationship, I have little connection to this man, nor will I ever know him. I turn back to my friends, and as I do so I can feel how very flushed my face is. I don't even know the first thing about him. The other kids in our family don't spend tons of time with him either, but for some reason, with them it's different. They say "Oh, he's just Malcolm. Don't spend so much time thinking about it." But as the youngest, no matter how hateful and critical I feel, I also have this sense that I'll always be the wholly insignificant kid sister. He may be a jerk, but if he'd just ask me how I'm doing or call me just to say hi, or if he ever said anything gooey, I might be inclined to look the other way.

"Wow," Doug remarks. "That was fast."

"He's pretty uptight," says Ray.

"But he is really cute," Rachel and Lila point out. The subject is dropped, and we go on to really important things like arguing over the actual benefits of living in Brooklyn and so on.

. . .

I spend Christmas with my mother and my other siblings. It's fun for about fifteen hours, and then I find myself sleeping a lot and checking my answering machine. On Christmas morning, the phone rings. Mom answers. It's Malcolm. She speaks very quickly and very quietly, and I can see tears streaming down her face. She hangs up the phone and stares ahead.

"Well?"

"That was your brother."

"Clearly."

"They had the baby."

"And?"

"It's a little girl."

"Whoops. There goes the line."

Whereupon my sister Meg chimes in: "And it'll be whelped in the spring, right?"

"Be nice, girls."

"And do you want to know what they named it?" my mother asks gravely.

"Jesus?" I inquire.

"Well, as a matter of fact, I thought you'd be interested to note that they've decided to call her Elizabeth."

dog days of august

* * *

So only after I'd dropped off my dog for his three-week summit at L.A.'s Animal Behavior Transformation Center did I become more fully acquainted with the world of modern medicine. The Animal Behavior Transformation Center is a solo operation run by a man who bears a striking resemblance to Ed Harris in very high heels. That is to say, if Ed Harris were to sport heels—not pumps, exactly, but manly, stacked, unseen heels—he might come to resemble Albert, my dog rehabilitator. Who is six feet three inches of squinting, chakra-aligning, holistic dog-training prowess. With those sky blue eyes found only in healers and I suppose members of the Third Reich's High Command. And he wears only those nondecorated white long-sleeved T-shirts that look cool exclusively on dog trainers and surfers, and you know this because every time you thought someone *else* looked cute in a long-sleeved T-shirt, the second he turned his back you were also presented with a graphic listing of every stop on Cheap Trick's U.S. reunion tour. Not Albert.

Who came promptly to meet me and collect my misbehaving Jack Russell terrier at Laurel Canyon Dog Park before taking him to his home, which happens to be the Animal Behavior Transformation Center. A friend had warned me that this guy really could read minds, and that he would know instantly if I thought he was a jerk. When I first laid eyes on him I tried to banish these thoughts. Unfortunately I stumbled through my own thought exorcism and wound up actually playing a kind of mental game of chicken with myself. (In seconds I was acutely conscious of thinking the thought "What if I thought he was a jerk" even though I *wasn't* actually thinking it.) Plus, when I shook his hand I suddenly wished that I had worn slightly more appealing clothes and didn't look quite so much like Gilligan. I can't do that I-just-came-from-the-gym routine that so many people do because I do not own clothing with the appropriate chevrons and spice stripes that other people wear to indicate this, particularly since I don't *got back,* and also because I resigned from the West Hollywood Crunch when I came to the profound realization that it's better to endure the Bataan Death March that is Runyon Canyon at midday than to find oneself tripping on a treadmill sandwiched between Tobey Maguire and Mena Suvari.

So I am chatting with Albert and wondering if there is any way he will regard the enormous safety pin holding my eyeglasses together as a cool political statement about the *need to mend,* when he gazes at me, touches my shoulder, and asks, softly, like they do, just what I thought had brought me into his energy. When I answer, "Your flyer at Petco," he instantly recognizes that I am almost entirely devoid of deeper understanding. I explain that my dog is a bright, alert, frequently charming, high-functioning creature who exhibits mysterious and terribly explosive outbursts of rage and depression wherein he snarls like a dybbuk in a bear trap. But who has a tremendous heart. And Albert says he could spend three weeks with *me* and probably know exactly what's wrong with my dog. This I initially regard as non-sense, then it seems just plain weird and unwarranted, and finally it morphs into a pretty good guess by a random char-latan with possibly valid instincts. Who happens to be slightly hot. And I begin to wonder just who the hell this guy thinks he is. But for now it's all about my dog, and I decide that once this three-week campaign of Shock and Paw is complete, we can deal with the other things.

As I drive home from the dog park, I am already missing my dog but I am now aware that something else is definitely wrong. I turn on the radio, though suddenly I'm unable to muster the cool struggle for appreciation required by NPR.

Nor can I play the brand-new iPod affixed to my car's tape deck, because I've never been able to put songs into it. When this problem initially arose, I went straight to the Apple store at Los Angeles's newest tranquil shopping cen-ter, the Grove. Where the salesgirl took the iPod away and told me to go kill time. So I dutifully spent the next hour dodging people I know at this eerily modern outdoor mall that's trying to look like a piazza complete with gracious computer-controlled fountains and a jingling Stepfordian trolley. When I returned to the store, the girl said my iPod was now working, and that she'd even put a bunch of songs on it that she thought I'd like, absolutely free of charge. Which delighted me until I looked at the playlist and noticed they were all songs with Christian titles like the hip-hop version of "Christ My Savior Be Thine." Shocked, I told her gently that I did attend church regularly and that I did have Jesus in my life but that I didn't want Jesus on my iPod.

So that's why I am driving home in silence on the way back from the dog park. Next thing I know there are hot tears in my eyes. And out of nowhere I'm wondering where some touchy-feely healer guy gets off implying that maybe I'm connected to my dog's neuroses. Which is when all of the liquid drains from my throat and mouth. And suddenly I am freezing and I don't even have air-conditioning and my anxiety literally forces me off the road, and I sit shivering. And finally give credence to the arrogant person's worst nightmare—what if someone else has a good point? And it dawns on me that perhaps all of my posturing is just that—and that maybe Albert knows something I don't and that maybe my arrogance about the value of things like mind readers and healers and Shania Twain is just defensiveness on the part of a bright, alert, high-functioning, occasionally charming aphid like me.

And I begin to feel dizzy, and then suddenly I know what Albert's place, the Animal Behavior Transformation Center, looks like. It will be in some spectacular cul-de-sac in Topanga Canyon. And I know instantly that when I enter his home I will be inside an extraordinary candlelit sanctuary, where I'll be greeted by a few serene parrots and maybe an Emmy winner's abandoned pig lounging languidly. I will head out back to where Albert is likely to be helping a border collie log onto AOL while he strokes a formerly rabid pit bull on whose belly a tiny kitten now resides. I am sure Albert's own dog (who will be a mottled, scarred, certified therapy dog) will greet me cheerily like some Hollywood development executive's assistant, smiling boisterously before asking if I want water, Diet Coke, cappuccino, or a career before his boss finishes with a call. And there will be soothing music on the stereo, and it might be from India and it might be Massive Attack, but it will not matter. And Albert will emerge, and he will hand me green tea, which will no longer be repellent to me, and he will ask me if I want to accompany him on yet another rescue operation—this time to save a nest of baby golden eagles whose mother has been killed by a logger. And I will ask Albert why he does these things, and he will say with genuine humility that it's his role in life. And he will ask what my role in life is, and I will admit that it is to complain and criticize and resent my agents. And then a pair of once-injured rabbits will come and settle in my lap and look lovingly up at me, just happy to be near me. And I will know that I am safe.

I don't mind things that are holistic. I've bought candles without feeling superior, edgy, or ironic. In fact, as a child I frequently held marshmallows impaled on a twelve-inch grilling fork high above our formal dining room candles in order to toast them, until I realized that it was far easier to toast them with gardening gloves over a Bic lighter. Which I did until the day my sister shrieked at me that I could get butane poisoning and my brother told her politely to shut the hell up because having his kid sister go up in a firestorm of butane wouldn't be such a terrible thing.

I finally start up my car and return to Mulholland Drive startled and teary, unable to explain it. Within three hours I have made an appointment with a psychiatrist in Westwood about adjusting my psychotropic-medication levels. Since my regular old psychotherapist is off spending my hard-earned Unemployment dollars in Quogue for August. The Unemployment—to which I am entirely brand-new—had felt weird until the fifty-seventh unemployed actor I knew reminded me I had technically earned it, that everyone did it at some time, and that it was essentially the Man giving something back. Of course this federally funded proof of failure became more searingly unpleasant when I revealed it to my mother. She'd phoned that morning to ask if I knew this Kobe Bryant fellow, since we'd grown up in the very same town.

"Um, no, Mom. Kobe Bryant is about fourteen."

"Oh. Well, in that case perhaps you might want to meet Frank and Barbara O'Leary's son. He lives in San Diego, and he's just about your age." (The "in that case" part did make me wonder if she had initially hoped I might somehow *reconnect* with Kobe Bryant.)

That would be fine, I told her, marveling at her newfound espousal of what was obviously a Catholic boy.

"Apparently he's adorable. And you never know, Lamb-

chop, sometimes those mackerel-snappers can really surprise you."

I opted to tell her about my unemployment. She paused
before asking me how long I expected to receive these *government disability checks,* and I told her I was sure they'd cease
as soon as I got some freelance work. Or the minute I got
called up for another tour in Nam.

The next day I'm off to see Dr. Kopelman. Who is over in
that faux part of Westwood by UCLA that thinks it's Har-
vard Square with its matrix of multicultural kids shuttling
back and forth between Starbucks and other Starbucks.
This doctor is nice. Married to another doctor who shares
his office suite. They hail originally from Boston, which
I know is a major medical center for major medical per-
sonnel, but I can just tell they are the kind of people who
practiced in Boston, then one weekend checked out New
Hampshire because it looked like fun to hike there and then
immediately moved their twin Subarus there full-time because of the tax benefits. And Dr. Kopelman is lovely and
he does make a bridge with his hands and he listens to me
explain the situation about my medication's new side ef-
fects. When my take-the-edge-off pills were prescribed two
years prior, I was told that most people should expect three
speeds: calm, active, and exuberant. The speeds I had recently experienced were fetal, more fetal, and blue rage.
Unless I have a glass of red wine, which makes me overtly
maudlin, curiously patriotic, and quite likely to sleep with

whatever nationality and species I'm with. I do not tell Dr. Kopelman that recently I have been startled to learn that not everyone writes the invisible word *help* on a guy's shoulder blades during unfulfilling sex, as I have done for years. He smiles and says I am a fascinating case study. I ask if he should admit this to a patient. Then he asks if I have trouble distinguishing between right and wrong. I say "occasionally." I do not tell him that as a child, I honestly believed that God kept a tally board. Not a tally board about whether you were naughty, nice, or bound for eternal damnation, but one that posted the results of every argument you've ever been involved in. His own scoreboard that listed the real winners. Each time there was screaming and yelling and parents said, "We'll talk about it later" or "You're both being silly," God knew, in His own little racetrack-handicapping way, just who had actually won the fight. Thus I was often possessed of a sudden calm, frequently misinterpreted to be a Gandhi-ish stance of maturity but in actuality a rather arrogant belief that once inside the pearly gates, it would be clear that I had triumphed repeatedly. So we spend an hour talking about why I have so much trouble sleeping, focusing, and parking, before he writes me a new prescription.

Within two weeks I begin to sleep past 4 A.M., and I no longer spend hours considering the plaster on my ceiling. Within another three days I can actively tolerate people with jobs, husbands, and recurring roles. The drugs are working. But of course you can't say that your new calm is courtesy of Eli Lilly, so I attribute it all to green tea, lower carb intake, and my holistic dog trainer. And when I go to pick up my dog, I drive along, eager and nervous to see what the Animal Behavior Transformation Center really looks like. And worried that Albert will see through my new medicated haze of clarity. Will he know that an additional twenty-five milligrams of anything really can make a difference? Will he want me? And so caught up am I by what Albert will think that I don't even notice that his directions aren't actually to Topanga Canyon. And that the Animal Behavior Transformation Center isn't actually a candlelit oasis in which happy animals live. Rather, the Animal Behavior Transformation Center turns out to be a tiny one-bedroom apartment with shag carpeting nestled behind an ill-designed mall known euphemistically as the West Side Pavilion. When I enter and find no border collies, no squirming kittens, and no candles, only Chinese food containers, muddy sneakers, and my exuberant dog jumping out of his skin to go home—but doing so politely—I look at Albert. He smiles and says, "I think your dog's gonna be all right now." And he turns and enters his kitchen. I watch him go and also suddenly notice, emblazoned across his back, every one of Korn's 2004 summer tour dates. But as I scoop up my dog and head out to the car, that doesn't matter so much.

venice

. . .

A few years ago I was writing promotional copy for a special-edition DVD release of that film *The Wings of the Dove* for a highbrow magazine to which I contribute regularly. My mind drifted to some of the more topical and relevant questions my friends and I frequently posed to one another— our favorite being: *For a million dollars would you cut off your pinkie toe?* or, *For ten million dollars would you agree to walk with a limp for the rest of your life?*—before I began simply to ponder basic Life Questions like *If you heated up ketchup, would you have tomato soup or at least sauce?* and so on. I knew I really absolutely had to return to the project at hand, but the phone rang. It was my friend Alexandra, from college, who is the editor of a celebrated teen fanzine and who tends to call me every single morning in order to play this brief word game we like. A frivolous, diversionary thing with movie titles. That we love, but that bores everyone else silly.

"Hey," Alexandra said. "What are you doing?"

"Writing," I tell her. "Nothing."

"Okay. A tiny mouse finds himself in a screen adaptation of Broadway's smash musical about a plant and a dentist—"

"Stuart Little Shop of Horrors!" I said.

"Nice. What happens when you put Angelina Jolie in a New York City sublet with Richard Dreyfuss and Marsha Mason?"

"The Goodbye Girl, Interrupted."

"Good."

"All right. Alex. Sigourney Weaver plays a primate specialist who travels to a seaside Connecticut town and meets local girl Julia Roberts who—"

"Gorillas in the Mystic Pizza!"

"Well done, Al. And now, this Hitchcock locomotive thriller with a creepy double murder gets derailed when Ewan McGregor shows up with a lot of heroin—"

"Strangers on a Trainspotting!" she shouts.

"Sympatico."

"Gotta work. Bye. "

"Me too. Bye."

And it was done. The daily call takes less than three minutes, ably demonstrating that my friends and I have some serious focus issues and/or have way too much time on our hands. I looked at the clock, and *whoops,* I needed to smoke a cigarette. Which would require a brisk and vigorous apartment scouring. My quarry (of the Ultra Light Filter variety) found in an unused raincoat pocket, I got down to the task at hand. Which was *The Wings of the Dove.* I struggled for a while and finally wrote about the movie by saying that *Helena Bonham Carter, the Holly Golightly of the Merchant-Ivory set, fi-*

nally bares all, emotionally and otherwise, in this new film based on the Henry James work. I felt it unnecessary to comment further about the tone of Henry James's story, or about its inevitable ending, since it seemed to me that absolutely *nothing* that Henry James did ended without lots of people being left stranded, shattered, or longing—and in most cases, all three. In fact, as I had learned haplessly stumbling through prep school before my eventual expulsion, nobody seemed to like Henry James at all, although I am willing to admit that our entire curriculum may have been damaged by a rather unfortunate ritual undertaken by the upperclassmen. At the beginning of each semester they would secretly confiscate all of the ninth-graders' English books and jot the endings down on the inside of the book jacket, thus greatly diminishing—and frequently ruining—their impact. I remember inside of Richard Wright's *Black Boy* someone had written "A cat gets hanged in this story," and in Stendhal's *The Red and the Black* I found scribbled in blood red ink, "They never have real sex and he dies." Inside *Crime and Punishment*, I recall, "This Distavski guy is *totally* hilarious. Tell your parents to buy you *all* his funny books to read over spring break." Even *Catcher in the Rye*, which a lot of people seemed to like, did not escape this fate. Inside my copy a senior had written one word: "Poseur." Sometimes they would just mislead us entirely. In *The Scarlet Letter* someone wrote: "The girl's a whore. The *A* stands for *adultery*, stupid. And she gets torn apart by a bunch of African jackals in the end." And in *Ethan Frome*: "They don't ever hook up. They're both losers. This story is a waste of time. But the sledding part is excellent, until her neck snaps off." F. Scott Fitzgerald wasn't immune either: "Jay Gatsby is really a fag, that's why he has all those clothes and he won't marry Daisy. He and Nick are doing it through this whole dumb book."

We were eternally frightened of upperclassmen in boarding school. They always stood around after dinner smoking cigarettes on the football bleachers, taking sips from small flasks whose contents inspired fear, wonder, and unabashed awe among my classmates. Once I ventured shyly over to a boy whose tattered clothing was, I later discovered, an elaborate attempt to defuse rumors that his father was the very corrupt and very rich Labor Minister of Belize. I boldly asked him for a cigarette, and he'd snarled that maybe I'd prefer some "hootch." I replied that while I didn't like hootch at all, I'd be happy to try some of whatever was in his flask, whereupon I was banished from the bleachers amid peals of laughter, never to return.

Taking matters into our own hands, the following semester my roommate and I opted to mix several ounces of Southern Comfort, Bacardi 151, black plum liqueur, an airplane bottle of Crown Royal, Tab, and Orange Shasta. We'd smuggled the alcohol back from Christmas vacation in Bonne Bell Ten-O-Six face cleanser and Vidal Sassoon shampoo bottles. She and I based our activity on Mary Poppins's "spoonful of sugar" theory, and we set about mixing the spirits in the shocking-pink bucket whose former purpose had been to hold our soap, toothpaste, and shampoo. We drank it out of Dixie cups. Then we chased the mixture with tap water and listened to *Breakfast in America* twice, the

B side of *Abbey Road* four times, the "Suite: Judy Blue Eyes" single six times nonstop, a Neanderthal Loggins and Messina bootleg I'd stolen from my sister, and a very scratched Velvet Underground album we couldn't even begin to fathom. And before we lost operational vision and sensation in our limbs, my roommate had confided to me a shattering experience.

I should preface this by saying that my roommate was completely obsessed with ballet. She'd seen *The Turning Point* seven times and had sixteen glossy photographs of Mikhail Baryshnikov glued above her Marimekko color-coordinated eiderdown. That, next to the ubiquitous poster of Matisse's dancing people that always reminds you of a vaguely cultlike (but colorful) ritual. I'd also been bitterly resentful of her matching linens, because my siblings and I had been forced to use our father's U.S. Navy regulation scratchy wool blanket and non-Scandinavian plain white cotton sheets (clearly woven by somebody of Laura Ingalls Wilder's vintage). Nor did they have the cool fitted corners that were the rage in 1979.

I knew nothing about the ballet, but I did know that my roommate had an older brother who was bad news, so the event that she recounted that happened seven years prior made perfect and horrifying sense to me. It had been the evening of her seventh birthday, and her parents had taken my roommate and her brother to a gala performance of *The Nutcracker*. As soon as the Mouse King came onstage, her brother had instructed her to stand on her seat (third row center, orchestra) and yell out *"Bitch Mouse!"* at the top of her lungs for all of the New York City Ballet patrons to hear. She had been whisked instantaneously from the theater, but not before disrupting the entire show and suffering what must have been a shattering loss of innocence.

Hearing this story, I told her that this was not the first time I had tried liquor. I explained how in Salzburg, Austria, in 1970, my siblings had taken it upon themselves to provide that illuminating experience for me.

I was five, and my mother and father had opted to take all the kids derived from multiple marriages on a six-week whirlwind tour of Europe. One evening, they wanted a night out alone, and they'd asked the big kids if they'd look after Elizabeth. Given my teenaged siblings' various pro-clivities, the kids had any number of things they'd rather have done, including having their own night on the town without the parents. Feeling trapped into responsibility, they realized that the answer to their problems lay in alco-hol. No sooner had my mother and father headed out than my eldest brother was apparently dispatched to the local liquor store to purchase a jug of the most robust and potent wine he could find. One sister marched down to the concierge, where she politely inquired whether there were any other children staying at our pension, on the theory that it would be fun to meet some other kids. She was promptly ushered by an unsuspecting bellhop to room 604, where an Italian couple was staying with their six-year-old son. My sister (clad in a frilly Austrian dirndl and pink Converse All-Stars with her hair in lengthy marigold braids) managed to evoke a playful kind of American goodness. It didn't hurt that she described in depth her kid sister's extremely lonely five-year-old status and her deep and genuine commitment to finding me somebody "nice" and "safe" to play with. Nowadays I cannot imagine any family handing over their child like that, but she was so convincing, and I suppose 1970 was such an innocent era, that after about twenty minutes the parents somehow agreed to relinquish their boy to this beaming dutiful blonde. She took the boy and returned to our rooms, where my other siblings had converged to hold me hostage at command central. The boy, Gino, and I were introduced, and all the big kids went about arranging lots of games for the two of us. Finally my brother Eliot returned with the wine. Whereupon, the kids told us that the contents of this jug would only make us play the games better and make us *see magical fairies like Bullwinkle and Top Cat really quick.* Then there was some talk about how they were off to buy us some more special "treats," and when they returned, *Gino and I better have drunk a lot more of the special fun bug juice!*

Needless to say, despite my penchant for 6 A.M. bounds out of bed, I was not awake for the carnage that took place the following morning involving my extremely ticked-off parents, Gino's horrified, lawsuit-threatening family, and the mortified concierge. Once they had pumped Gino's stomach (I had somehow been spared this intestinal assault) and my siblings were grounded, I got to ride around in solitary splendor viewing the many wonders of Salzburg. And while the entire episode was forgotten, I was naturally leery of booze for the next several years.

My roommate and I considered our mutual revelations carefully, before eking out the smile that is the first sign of ironic memory and maybe even nostalgia in a fourteen-year-old. Then we forgot about the incidents entirely, hid the bottles, and raced outdoors to get some fresh air and hunt down the hoagie/grinder sandwich truck in an attempt to absorb some of the ethanol solvents aswish in our stomachs. And it was these events I recalled as I stared blankly at my *Wings of the Dove* copy, whereupon I deleted the paragraph I had written and wrote simply "Appealing actors, great clothes, adequate story line, pretty scenery, crappy ending."

the examination

. . .

Here's what I learned over the summer about the power of perception, revenue documentation, and my mother.

Because even when you relocate to Southern California and you have previously unimagined opportunities to re-invent yourself, you can still blow it. You're just tan and probably wearing shorts when you do so.

After the pleasant lady from the IRS with the unpro-nounceable name and the legislative power to imprison me phoned to schedule my audit, the only thought that popped into my small and felonious skull was how I would tell my mother.

My mother, who had recently observed that by the time they were my age, Jack Kennedy, Mary Tyler Moore, and Jesus had all made some pretty big career moves and *when was I gonna be on the TV?*

So I picked up my ringing phone in the early-morning darkness, and of course it was Mother. She likes to call at 6:30 A.M. Pacific Time, because of that universal Mother's

Right to Wake the Spawn. She announced she was en route to the Naval War College in Newport, Rhode Island, to listen to the Joint Chiefs of Staff and the FBI Director talk about the state of affairs in the Middle East. And rather than ask her if she had actually won this trip on some Fox News Channel "Proud to Be an American" sweepstakes, I simply commented that it was probably a good thing for the Joint Chiefs of Staff that she would be in attendance. Although I could only hope that she might refrain from reminding the FBI Director that we'd grown up next door to his family in the gutless mix of adultery and tonic that is our hometown *and* that his parents' standard poodle had rather violently impregnated our own miniature poodle, who certainly hadn't seen it coming.

Then she asked if she'd woken me up.

"Nah, Mom. I was just doing some calisthenics before I board the cargo plane headed for Camp Lejeune."

"You don't even know what Camp Lejeune is," she said.

So then she started in on George W. Bush, because she'd recently been to the White House for some ceremony to watch him give something away.

"Like Panama?" I asked her.

"No, silly," she said. "He gave a medal of commendation to the Undersecretary of Commerce." At that point God intervened on my behalf and her cell phone connection hit a rough patch somewhere around Mystic, Connecticut. When her reception came back in I knew I had to tell her about my audit, but I bought a vowel and some time by changing the subject to movies. Of course all she likes are the war pictures. Having seen *U-571* four times in the theaters, I knew she'd been all over *Windtalkers,* which had opened that week, even though she finds Nicolas Cage far too ethnic to represent any First World nation. So I primed the pump and we talked about *heroes* and *decency* and *America,* and onto that fertile patriotic soil I lobbed out the fact that I was about to be audited by her beloved government. There was a long pause, and finally Mom said, "Hmmm. You remember Burt Hayes." Well, of course I did.

When I was about nine my parents had a big black-tie dinner party, and I had been sufficiently bathed, primed, and nightie-clad to be presented, like a pink seersucker fortune cookie, to the guests to say good night before bed. And as I headed down the stairs into our formal living room I remember being mesmerized as Burton Hayes proposed a toast—completely oblivious to the half-eaten, sauce-covered cocktail shrimp protruding from the breast pocket of his dinner jacket. Mr. Hayes then offered a lavish tribute to his wife, who stood next to him, shivering like an eager whippet, curiously unfazed by the list of vulgar expletives, and the even more obscene nouns he used to depict her. And after each bad word the guests seemed to roar gleefully as if to say "Yes! She *is* that bad word, too!!" whereupon he would kiss her lustily to the accompanying applause. This had gone on for some ten minutes before the two of them collapsed in a heap on the floor laughing. Then he began to root around in his wife's hair and neck like a tuxedoed truffle hound, depositing sloppy kisses across her face as they writhed around on our shag carpet.

And it was only this physical display (not any other element of his performance) that prompted the guests to finally snort with good-natured disapproval and make him stop. He had from that moment onward always seemed to me to be the only person on the earth who was permitted—and actually encouraged—to use foul language in our hometown and nobody seemed to care. My mother—who typically wouldn't tolerate such language—looked upon him with a glazed expression, and I wondered why she hadn't told him to be quiet, as she had all of us when so much as a "damn" was uttered. But now she just watched, withstanding all obscenities, objecting only to the Hayeses' lurid physical antics. Which is when I realized that sometimes people let other people get away with things that aren't allowed.

So that's what I remembered about Burton Hayes.

"Yeah, sure, Mom, the man with the bad words. Of course I remember him. But what does Mr. Hayes have to do with my audit?"

Turned out that Burton Hayes had recently died from subacute bacterial endocarditis doing twenty-five years for tax fraud—after a botched audit—at a minimum-security prison in Ossining, New York.

Oh.

So there's *that.*

Although curiously, just when I thought Mother was going to start in on morality, ethics, life in the Big House, or my possible exile in Cuba, she suddenly announced that God and the U.S. government probably knew down deep that I was a good kid and if I wore a nice skirt, didn't swear, and told the truth, I'd be fine.

"So all right then. And get a move on. Time to rise and shine, Lovebug. You'll feel better if you do. *You're my special dragon and don't you forget it.*"

She signed off cheerily, having spied a HoJo's somewhere on I-95—"you know, with the good extra-crispy fried clam strips." And she was gone, racing up the Eastern Seaboard.

Over the next three months I remained in a state of deminausea as I awaited my IRS appointment on West Forty-fourth Street in Manhattan. What was most unsettling was that I wasn't entirely sure *why* I was being audited. I hadn't the faintest notion. Although I would soon discover that the fact that I was a writer who maintained two residences in two major metropolitan areas with no discernible income and whopping psychotherapy bills was a pretty big red flag.

But here's the thing. I learned Three Big Secrets about getting audited by the IRS that they won't tell you. That should be shared with anyone who's even vaguely considering throwing away a receipt.

The First Secret: when you're called, don't wait. Go at once. The Internal Revenue Service gives you three months to schedule your audit, which is not necessarily a good thing. Because even if that *sounds* like a good thing, three months can creep sickly along, so that you become like a medical patient waiting for test results. Thus by the time you actually arrive at your appointment so much time has elapsed that you are absolutely convinced that you will go to jail *and* that you have lymphatic cancer.

The Second Secret? Nice people you might hang around, date, or drink with and audition with get audited too. I learned this when I contacted my accountant in New York, a wily bond-crazy leprechaun who suddenly turned into a Dickensian parson when I told him about the audit. He pointed out repeatedly that anyone who didn't keep all her receipts was a "perfect moron." But here's the what. In the two months I waited to fly back to New York for the event, at least fourteen other "perfect morons" had emerged from the woodwork and told me about *their* audits. Happily and openly. *Nice* people. With appliances, grocery lists, and solid voting records. Which was, in its own way, quite comforting indeed.

So I flew to New York where my accountant told me that the IRS liked organization, efficiency, and thoroughness, and instead of reminding him that if I'd *possessed any of those qualities to begin with,* I probably wouldn't be getting audited, I got to work. I bought a three-ring binder complete with multicolored index dividers and prepared a twenty-two-page document that actually amounted to little more than a very pretty breakdown of the days of the month in multiple fonts, which, I had to admit, was most attractive if possibly useless. I found about 65 percent of my bank statements for the year 2000, as well as my datebook, which, if one wonders, is like gold. I removed all of my jewelry, nail polish, and anything that looked like it'd been purchased with American currency, receipt or not.

And on July 30 I met my accountant in the waiting room of the IRS's New York City headquarters. Which had clearly been designed by the production team behind *Monster's Ball*, filled with entirely nonthreatening officers languishing in khaki who showed me into the corral-style waiting area, where I sat. After a numbing wait, Jean Stapleton's long-lost twin sister beckoned me forward to meet my auditor, the pleasant lady with the unpronounceable name and the legal jurisdiction to imprison me—who actually bore a striking resemblance to J.Lo. Back we went to her cubicle. Which is when the IRS's Third Big Secret hit me. The Big What You See vs. What They See Secret. Where it becomes devastatingly clear that unless you're actually running an Indonesian sweatshop, an audit is all about perception. *It's financial smoke and mirrors.* Because once they set the hook, if you earnestly play it all out, you're probably going to be okay. And as this realization slowly dawned upon me, I began to tell J.Lo far more about my life and spending habits than she ever wanted to know. I talked and talked and talked. I became a relentless geyser of information, welcome or not. For the next four and a half hours we went through every meal, every head shot, every videotape, every movie ticket, every lunch date, and every gum wrapper I'd ever glanced at in my life.

And when I told her about how my church donations weren't necessarily recorded because I usually just put the money in the plate and scooted out before Communion, I think J.Lo was pretty convinced that I didn't have much to hide. And that is the secret of the IRS. As long as they see that they've humbled you and that you've done the work, you're probably going to emerge alive.

Two weeks later I received a letter from the IRS with the blessed words "No Change" on my federal income tax return. And while I wouldn't want to go through the process again, I remain touched by the fact that where families, money, and the government are concerned, perception is everything.

those snappy durable creatures

• • •

My mother had a tumor about the size of an external modem extracted from her lower intestine. A few months later my sister phoned me exasperated, demanding to know if Mother was "boldly *trying* to lure the cancer back into her abdomen or just defy us all."

At the time of Meg's distress call I happened to be back in New York for a week. And I'd been staring blankly at my computer screen, trying to write some freelance copy. As my dog furiously dug into a chenille throw on the couch in his endless quest to locate a rabbit or a badger somewhere in the apartment, I struggled to find another word for "green" that was gutsier than *pear,* although not as precious as *fern* or *peapod,* nor as weird as *lichen.*

"Meg, she's fine," I said. "What are you talking about?" Just then my dog's head popped jubilantly up from the chenille in that universal gesture of Quarry Found. He began to shake his head gleefully to break the neck of the Bic ballpoint between his jaws, which now fought gamely for its life.

Meg explained that just that morning Mother had cooked half a pound of bacon, Hollywood eggs, and scrapple.

"Can you believe this, Rodent? Do you know where scrapple comes from?"

"Heaven?" I'd offered.

"No, stupid, it's the . . . it's—it's pig debris."

I was going to ask Meg if she really meant *debris* or meant *detritus* or *flotsam* or *jetsam* or just *shards of their tiny satanic nonkosher hooves,* but I thought better of it and pointed out cheerfully that at least Mom was making Hollywood eggs for *somebody.* Since our dad had died she'd seemed devoid of purpose. We had all tried to get her to go out with men, but she seemed not to care much. She attended plenty of parties and knew tons of men but always remained incredibly traditional and frustratingly formal about it all. And she wouldn't budge on the "it's the man who must phone the lady" format.

"It's been five years now, Mom, you know, you could date," Meg said over Christmas, as I also stood there, nodding in complicity.

"Girls, this is not an *if/then* clause I will ever act upon," she had said. "That is not an option. Besides, you think I don't have my hands full with you two and your brothers running around, demanding this and proclaiming that?"

"We don't think you should just worry about *us* all the time," I said.

"Mom," said Megan, "of course you have your hands full. We just think you—"

"Ladies, let's not have this we-just-think or we-just-want-you-to-be-happy drill. I'm absolutely fine, and I do not wish to hear the *we-just-think*s until it is time to lift my ancient, palsied, wheelchair-bound body into a home."

Which every single person in our entire family knew would never, ever, happen. She would outlive us all.

Nor would she ever go gently into that rocking and doing-needlepoint-style dark night of widowhood. She's totally lucid, cogent, virulently right-wing, and an avid moviegoer.

Not long ago, I received the following e-mail:

Dearest Miss Pink:

I am told it is sunny in Los Angeles this morning. Perhaps next month it will rain and that way you will be able to discern what day it is.

Regards the cinema, just took myself off to see Almost Schmidt—I should think it might garner Nicholson an Oscar, tho' it is very depressing, the characters are remarkably played out and remarkably unattractive (I don't think we even know that many people who are that unattractive who have been in one place at the same time!)—but i am sure so true to life!!!!!

So my sister was all bent out of shape because Mom was eating sausage, scrapple, and other obscure foods too inexpensive to ever be labeled delicacies.

"She . . . she's—she's had cancer and she's eating garbage!"

Naturally I refrained from mentioning that for some it was, nevertheless, tasty garbage. Nor did I mention that our mother would probably be eating this garbage way past *all* of our respective deaths, and that at least Mother would be the most snappily dressed arthropod around. In fact, I went on to myself, when it comes to indestructibility, *sharks are the oldest and most durable creatures on earth*—they're basically prehistoric— and they're frequently found with tire irons, aerosol cans, and discarded windshield wipers in their stomachs. But rather than make clumsy comparisons between the GI tracts of Mother and most marine predators, I decided to keep quiet. Because I am the youngest child. I simply said to Megan, ten years my senior, that of course her concern was merited and that I would always support her. I had been offering unconditional support to my sister on the telephone for years. Hoping never to have to exercise it. Largely because her doings and concerns were so remote from my own, so impossibly well-intentioned and healthy compared with my sinful existence in the urban sprawl and sprawling urb that was Manhattan. Where I continued to thrive as a relatively happy arthropod myself. My sister wondered about how to better integrate the many children in her district's public school system. I wondered why public restroom hand dryers were so lame, and which conditioner left the least residue.

Also, in this age of conscientiousness, discipline, and DSL, just *letting somebody be* is rarely regarded as conscientious or thoughtful, let alone healthy. Yet I was convinced that if we let Mother be, she would be just fine. That she was one of those durable dry goods that would last a lifetime unaffected by conditions around her. Mother's body isn't a temple. It's its own fallout shelter.

I ruminated upon this as I sat at the bar of the Carlyle Hotel sipping a Bullshot waiting for Mother to return from the telephone. My sister had been lecturing to me about how we needed to be more responsible children, that Mother was fast approaching her second century and that nobody seemed worried about her.

Mother had arrived in New York that afternoon. And, despite her recent surgery (and what my sister now calls "Mom's Colon Cancer in Just 5 Days Diet"), Mother was absolutely determined to take her long-scheduled five-week trip to Mongolia. Just like that. And she'd appeared at Penn Station as usual, reeking of Protestant purpose, general disapproval, and Chanel No. 19.

Naturally I had been there to meet her. Since my father died, Mother had always asked if on the off chance that I happened to be, you know, in or around the neighborhood of (what she meant was loitering) Penn Station, which given my sometime theatrical pursuits I was, could I meet her when she arrived.

One of the uglier by-products of Philadelphia is the fact that when you leave it and are finally able to speed through the atmospheric layer back into Manhattan's orbit, you have to do it via Penn Station. Period. No matter how many times you stroll reverently through Grand Central, admiring its gracious supervision of the Almighty Commute, astonished by its scale and wondering what time they filmed that *Fisher King* waltz sequence, you'll never really be able to call it your port.

So I always went to meet her. She is not hard to miss amidst the teeming hordes disembarking from Amtrak's 1:26 train. Mother always travels in a navy blue blazer with a khaki below-the-knee-length skirt (which she'll admit proudly and quietly is *absolutely* a blend. *Always travel in permanent-press so you can just rinse it out in a hotel sink!*

Plus, she always wears a perfectly starched button-down shirt, a few baubles—usually a charm bracelet commemorating each of her children's birthdays—sensible flats, and the crowning touch, gloves. Regardless of the season, Mother travels in gloves. Navy blue kid gloves that are a constant source of horror to me.

"You're off the train, Mom," I had said to her that afternoon. "You can take the gloves off."

"Certainly not, Lambchop. I wear them when I'm traveling. And I'm still traveling."

Try as I did to point out that she was in Hell's Kitchen in ninety-four-degree heat, she insisted upon wearing them until we arrived at 1000 Park Avenue, at my ancient aunt's home, where Mother establishes her New York base camp. After this, we were off to lunch. Which is almost always at the Princeton Club, a perennial favorite. It is unchanging if moth-eaten, and hopelessly orange. It smells of prewar triumph, institutionalized brokerage, and good furniture wax. There are men wandering around in their rumply glen plaid suits whose hands always give off the faint and not un-pleasant odor of lemon and bourbon, who never tire of clapping other men on the back. There are men who have squinted into the sunlight of success and have never thought lives could be led any other way. Men who would no more put moisturizer on their skin, or wear wedding bands, than they would drink gasoline. Men who have all met heads of state, who all have children, who all have had affairs, and who would each finally acknowledge (but only in a doctor's office) that there is a God. Men who wouldn't dream of letting a woman pick up the tab under any circumstances, and who know Grand Central as well as their own closet. Men who loathed Bill Clinton like nobody's business, but who secretly applauded the man's shocking bravado among his interns. Men who play superb squash and have marched up Indonesian cliffsides, but who cower before the Internet.

So Mother was here to get her visa and documents organized for this trip to Mongolia. Why she had to go to Mongolia just five months after cancer surgery was beyond me. Why she had to come to New York City for her visa and passport validation was also a supreme mystery. Why couldn't she just send the stuff to the Mongolian Consulate instead of coming in person?

"Lambchop," she'd explained, "I like to do it in person; you know how the U.S. mails are."

But to be quite honest, I hadn't the slightest notion about what was wrong with the U.S. mails, or why they were so suspect. Still, I kept my mouth shut, figuring that Mother and Kevin Costner must have known something I didn't. So I acquiesced and traipsed along after her to the Chinese Consulate, conveniently located on Eleventh Avenue, where she took pains to point out that Red China—as she so archaically refers to it—was really a time bomb for the rest of us. Because, said she, "we've all been lulled into believing that the Communist threat is over—and that's exactly what those people want us to think." I eyed the Chinese employees suspiciously when we arrived, although I had a hard time believing any one of these simple earnest clerks was capable of spearheading some kind of global annihilation.

Then Mother insisted that since we were in the neighborhood, we needed to go look at the USS *Intrepid*—docked nearby—because it was important and, she said, *you're always going to be glad you know your way around an aircraft carrier.* An early (but eventually spurned) suitor of Mother's was rumored to have proposed to her somewhere near one of the ship's torpedo holds, which is another reason why we think she is so sentimentally attached to the Navy's seagoing vessels. That and the fact that if it were World War II all the time, our mother wouldn't mind it one bit.

With paperwork and aircraft-carrier visits complete, we returned to the apartment and my sister phoned for an update on Mother's health. Meg reminded me that it was good to worry. That evening we went out for dinner instead of theater, because Mother said she was disgusted with Broadway's current offerings. She announced that she wasn't going to see one more goshdamn Middle American play about people's ugly insides—what with characters sleeping with their own family members—and that until Pete Gurney wrote another something, we were sticking to movies. And as we went off to eat lobster and clams in drawn butter, she soon forgot about Broadway's blight.

The following afternoon I looked out the window as Mother's plane pulled away and headed toward Beijing. I had accompanied her to the airport, shared an enormous filet with creamed spinach and onion rings with her, listened to her describe the current political situation in Ulan Bator, listened to her ask for the hundredth time if there was *nothing* those Kennedys couldn't *buy, elect,* or *marry,* and, finally, listened as she ticked off the list of things we were to remember to do while she was wandering around on the steppes of Mongolia. And then she was off. Like she always is. And as I hopped into a cab I felt a teensy bit guilty, but of course, I really wasn't worried about a thing.

queens surface transport

· · ·

So I have returned to New York from Los Angeles for a week and I'm on my way out when Mother phones and she's got the movie section in front of her and she wants to know why on earth anyone would ever want to attend a filmed reenactment of a Greek wedding—mine, big, fat, or otherwise. And I point out that her own cultural outlook is just a few Ferragamo steps to the right of some of the militia members I hang out with, and then I tell her I'm going out. And she says *to where,* and I say *to the Tropical Rain Forest Exhibit at the Central Park Zoo,* and she says, "Oh. That's rich. Since when do you care about the rain forest?" To which I maturely reply, "Since now."

So I get to the Simulated Tropical Rain Forest Exhibit, where I've been planning to come for months. Because when you live in Los Angeles you spend, I think, an inordinate amount of time lamenting the time you're not in New York and then trying to figure out what that lamentation really *means* and does it mean that you actually miss it and do

you actually *belong* there, or are you just romanticizing it because you've got way too much time on your hands and
would you miss Cleveland, too, if you were tan, carbound,
and future-free? So you come back for a quick getaway and
suddenly you're crossing the avenues like *Yeah, I don't live here
anymore but make no mistake, I'm eminently qualified to give you directions
anywhere, like even to Proper Noun Streets in the West Village that I never
knew how to get to when I did live here.*

But the fact is I've been trying to get to the Simulated
Tropical Rain Forest Exhibit ever since I read the shattering
exposé in *The New York Times Magazine* about how we're all no
more than boomerang-tossing cannibals whose indifference has already pillaged our ever-diminishing wildlife
kingdom and how it all amounts to an environmental Ar-
mageddon just waiting to happen. So, time running out and
all, I decided to hightail it over to the nearest natural-
resource center, lickety-split, and check it out. That's what
happens when you notice essays in the *Times* Sunday magazine section right before the gratuitous ads for luxury
condos on Fifth and next to the weight-loss camp ads.

And I'm absentmindedly following a small square plac-
ard that details sleep patterns of red Amazon newts when
along comes this guy—one of those guys who think they're
going to tell you something you don't already know, like how
we should treat our environment like it's number one. The
kind of guy who you can just *tell* thinks he's got you figured
out like nobody's business, see, because here *you* are at the
Simulated Tropical Rain Forest Exhibit at the Central Park
Zoo, and he's noticed you've got glasses on, so you're prob-

ably not consumed by your own vanity. And he's also noted that given your yesterdecade clothes, you clearly aren't trying to pick anyone up, either. On the other hand, you're not with any children, so that means you came here alone, for your own *edification*. So he's thinking that means somehow you're interested in this sort of stuff.

And you instantaneously hate him for being so patronizing, and thinking he knows he's got your number dialed with that deliberately crooked John Cassavetes smile he offers like, *Hey, cool, here we are—two intelligent, educated people in a chance meeting at someplace other than a counter at Barney's or a fern-filled pastería on the Upper West Side,* and clearly he'd like to talk, but you despise his arrogance for reasons you don't fully understand.

And he's got that hip Jewish intellectual thing working, with the rumpled corduroys and the sturdy shoes and *The New York Review of Books* under his arm and a T-shirt peeking out beneath a button-down that has either the periodic table of elements or somebody Live at Red Rocks on it, and he knows that's exactly the kind of thing that just sucks you right in.

And he's got that literary bent that means it took him five years to graduate because there was so much Goddamn *fun* to be had in New Haven, and that kind of thing just spells trouble for you, and you tell yourself you've absolutely got to steer clear of this Tom Wolfe in sheep's clothing . . . and as he's approaching, you know with a kind of morbid warmth that he's the kind of guy who says his favorite thing about New York is the free movies in Bryant Park. And you know he'd take a bullet for Saul Bellow or Martin Amis, and he'd tell you Janeane Garofalo hung the moon and that John Sayles is civilization's only hope, and that he knows exactly the right moment to say David Foster Wallace was *over* but you also know he's got a big picture of Natalie Merchant on his cork bulletin board right next to a pair of tickets to hear Norman Mailer and Bono argue with Charlie Rose at the 92nd Street Y. You know that even though he says he watches out for Shark Week on the Discovery Channel he is also acutely aware of precisely *when* to confide that *Behind the Music* was groundbreaking, when it was coasting, and when it got important again. He's also exactly the kind of guy who says he thinks Catherine Keener's really remarkable and she's got such an apt mind, but he doesn't know why he's so wild about her, and you hate him for categorically denying that it has anything to do with the fact that she's also stunning to look at.

And you know that he always asks for soba noodles *off the menu,* and that he used to live with a guy in the East Village who played bass in a band that was just called "band" and that he'd happily tell you California's *only* noteworthy because it gave us citrus and made *option* a verb. And he's strolling over to get a better look at the Chilean salamander but that's because he just wants to chat, maybe tell you about how he likes books too, but how he thinks reading groups are *deuxième.* And that he'd say he'd rather swallow two hundred Coke-can tabs than sit through the World Premiere of an Important New Anything, and you're getting really woozy now and all you can think of are the horrible whirlpools that faced Ulysses, but if you tell him that, he'll just ask if you meant Homer or James Joyce and you hate him even more. And you want to smack him and tell him you've never even *seen* a John Sayles picture but that *Chicken Run* was a fine film, and he's getting even closer and sure he'll smile understandingly if you tell him you've never had the intellectual stamina to finish an issue of *The New Yorker* but you can't can't *can't* talk to this guy because you've been to that fire before, so you turn on your heel and you get the hell out of the Simulated Tropical Rain Forest Exhibit at the Central Park Zoo.

Relieved, you walk out into the sprawling urb that is Manhattan. With your dignity intact. Or at least some semblance of pride. You think. And so what if he was impossibly attractive—you can't think about things like that, you don't know why exactly, but someone this week said concentrate on yourself. Like maybe your mother and your grocer and every medical professional you know. And besides, you've noticed bright green gum on your shoe and you'd really like to know how long it's been there. So instead, at that very moment, an eerie manic cloud wells up inside of you and you suddenly become extremely annoying. You wander around arrogantly and pompously, feeling holier than thou and weighted with a greater sensitivity, a more refined angle, you think, on just about everything. You shamelessly lament your own idleness, calling it ennui but unable to spell it. But, it turns out, you're an idiot. Your job appalls you. Sure, you're a writer, but you really just create junk mail. You are the devil's script doctor. Which isn't even neat in an archival sort of way.

And then because you've got way too much time on your hands you suck your friends into that vortex. Your friends who in seconds begin to seem monochromatic because you've begun to shift blame. You've incarcerated them all into two categories from which, naturally, they'll never escape. Since clearly *you're* the only person around who can simultaneously take in both forest and trees.

On the one hand are your friends who, out of their own timid need to function safely within a system, have day jobs. Who see the day's variety in a hand roll or a quesadilla or maybe a new *font,* who personally feel and appreciate the impact voice mail has had upon society, who speak of hybrid engines, Clay Aiken, and refinancing opportunities in the same earnest commuter's breath. These people who have legitimately realized the dreams of an honest wage and who have secured Ayn Rand's place among other prophets who would correctly herald some neo-fascist world you hoped you would be too long gone to see. Where working humans are no more than sightless sandwich boards, leading driver's-side air-bag types of lives. These are your friends with jobs.

Then there are your colleagues in the other camp, who work sporadically. Or not at all. Who actively take advantage of a nation that, through no fault of its own, has economic systems whereby someone can simultaneously carp about and defend menial part-time work while they struggle to "make a difference" artistically. Those who actually feel they have some kind of right to preen their aesthetic pinfeathers in front of an adoring and guileless world, a world sucked in by its own earnest appetite for comfort through variety.

And it's these people who disgust you as you walk along, making a mental note of the Body Shop's animal-testing protest and Showtime's latest billboard foray into Message Movies, existing in and of the world as a kind of moral lightning rod . . . you capricious, infatuated, imperiously cross-eyed testament to narcissism. You who humble yourself to acknowledge the man who sells you cigarettes while you sip coffee with people in the morning under humid, greasy lights.

Suddenly you think about the people in your life who possess any complex regard for hifalutin misfits like James Joyce. You think about his smoldering, drunken Irish heart. And how infrequently people like that get deposited upon this earth. And then you think about Thomas Merton. Once you remember who he is. And you think yourself incredibly highbrow for thinking about Thomas Merton in the first place, and then you quickly, greedily, heap lots of other demi-important figures onto your shiny, horrifying plate and you swallow heartily, contentedly.

And then because you have nothing better to do you silently mouth words like *assiduous* and *bucolic* and *cypher*—for no particular reason other than the solid, powerful thud they make rappelling off the wall of your gums. And you continue on in your hatefully superior day, you unctuous, benevolent light shedder.

Which is when you step out confidently onto Madison Avenue searching vainly for significant meaning with which to begin a candid narrative in your bored and loathsome mind. And no sooner have you sleepily regarded all of these dull prospects than you see the large Queens Surface Transport bus bearing down upon you at forty miles an hour and accelerating. A huge, daunting, and very evil bus, with the coldest halogen eyeballs you've ever seen, and you can hear it getting louder and *louder, and it isn't like you can't move but like you don't move.* You don't move. And *sure* your heart is propelled from your chest cavity into your throat. And *sure* you can feel that funny liquid coating the edge of your eyeballs. And *here's* where you might say, "And now my troubles are finally over." But you won't. Because nothing happens. Nothing. You instinctively, mechanically step backward. One step. Averting disaster. Averting *Does what's left of the body have any identification on it?* Averting *This is EMS one-twenty-seven, we've got a dismembered female at East Fifty-eighth Street and seven witnesses.* Averting *And to think I just had a drink with her last night.* Averting *Gosh, I wish I'd gotten that green mock turtleneck back before she . . . is it absolutely* not cool *to ask her grieving family for it back?* Averting *This is Mrs. Raines from the credit office of Citibank Visa it's very important that you return my call at 1-800-763-0470.* You just take a step backward. And you live. And you live. And you're standing on the corner shaking and you're wondering about this near fatality and along comes the guy from the Simulated Tropical Rain Forest Exhibit at the Central Park Zoo and he stops in front of you and he bends down and he picks up your scarf, which has fallen onto the pavement, and he smiles and steadies you under your elbow and asks if you'd like to have a cuppa joe to calm down and all you can do is just stare at him and . . . and . . . and . . . nod, and mutely follow.

natural history

. . .

Six days before Christmas at the Museum of Natural History, surrounded by four-thousand creeping tourists, three reluctant siblings, two sobbing nieces, and dripping in the apple juice that one angry toddler had flung my way seconds prior, I suddenly realized that my father was really and truly dead. He'd been gone for a year, and it hadn't really hit me until that moment.

Mother was complaining that if only we'd remembered to bring the Museum Membership Thingee we wouldn't have had to pay so much *damn money to get in* and *they must be making money hand over fist here* and *who in creation ever heard of paying four dollars for a bottle of water in the first place.* I assured her that all museums were really hurting these days what with all the arts funding cuts and stuff, although I hadn't the faintest notion if that was actually the case.

"Speaking of which," she said, "I'm not exactly thrilled that all that tax money I kick in goes to paying for *fledgling Latin artists who piddle into bottles with the Baby Jesus inside.* Honestly.

That one makes our old drinkie bird Jackson Pollock look like the Angel Gabriel."

I pointed out that fifty years prior this *same* arts funding was paying for Edward Hopper's desolate landscapes, too.

"Mom," I said, "we can't pick and choose. If our nation's going to foot the bill to exhibit Winslow Homer's Bermuda vacation homes, we also have to foot the bill for what you so charitably refer to as *fledgling Latin artists.*"

"Well, that fella *was* Latin, wasn't he?" she asked.

My sister chimed in that maybe Mom was being just a teensy bit bigoted, and that maybe we shouldn't refer to the artists quite so ignorantly in public places.

Mother said, "Meggie, what the hell are you talking about? I just said he was a *Latin*. It's not as though I called him a *domestic.*"

The Christmas art-and-culture tour had become an annual event for the kids and grandchildren. We continued even after my dad passed away. Personally, I disliked these junkets intensely, but of course I like conflict less. So every year, I accompany my family because that's what Mom says one ought to do. After all, she always says, we were all just as lucky as we could be, *and we'd better damn well be gracious and cheery and think about somebody else for a change.* Thus I always bite my tongue and go.

So we hadn't even gotten past the "You Are Here" booth and Mother was ranting about how poorly the museum staff managed what they must have *known* would be holiday over-flow. "You know," she said, "when I was a little girl coming here—" and my brother chimed in that when she was a little girl coming here Thomas Edison was still working out the kinks and the animals in the display cases were still gazing down the barrels of the guns that would bring them here. My sister Meg then stormed off, explaining that she much preferred to explore the mysteries of the Nairobi Plain than endure another second of our very own Miss Anita Bryant.

The fact that our dad had died exactly one year earlier made everyone just a little more anxious. A quiet, studious man who favored bow ties and loafers, he was the kind of guy whose pockets could always be counted on to contain several quarters, a roll of mints that would withstand any and all carbon-dating processes, and a working pen. He hadn't liked loud or obstreperous people; how he managed to have married my mother, spawned me, and actually stick with any of us seems inconceivable now. He didn't really care for small talk. He was measured, balanced, and thoughtful, and therefore frequently overlooked. When he did speak, you always noticed it like you would an unusual but not un-pleasant breeze picking up across the way.

Our dad had always hoped in vain that we'd take more of an interest in the world around us. And that somehow our mother's penchant for parties and the overwhelming pres-ence of some of our slightly famous and extremely right-wing relatives might not subsume us entirely. On Saturday mornings, if no one looked particularly busy, he would suggest a family outing. Even when it rained, and my brother Malcolm grudgingly agreed to play bocce with me in the upstairs hallway, Dad would suggest a lecture on Canada Goose Migration Patterns at the nearby Audubon sanctuary. When nothing appealed, Dad was more than content to head off to the local library or bookshop to do research on one of the several books he published, like his text on Sociopathic Anxiety and Gender Disorders and Their Measured Influence Upon Psychotic Personality Development.

Our Christmas arts tour included several museum exhibits for the small fry with a little theater thrown in for Mother's four grown children. She deferred always to my brother Malcolm for suggestions on theater—the fact that I had now been moonlighting as a New York actor for some time made absolutely no difference to anyone whatsoever in the decision-making process. Malcolm called the shots. Malcolm was a walking testament to latter-day Aryan Supremacy—a man all too happy to condemn liberal elements of society, gangsta rap, and me.

I found that as I grew older I'd become more of a pill, and I took to making strategic hypodermic remarks to destabilize Mother's rosy world. Not out of any malice, but to make her realize that it wasn't all quite like Dwight Eisenhower and Ronald Reagan had said it would be. For example, that week we had taken the grandchildren to the Forbes Galleries to see the Fabergé eggs, which were—I thought—testament to a lifestyle she had no business endorsing for my six- and eight-year-old nieces. Thus, when Mom detailed the part where the Bolsheviks had systematically murdered the Czar's family, I explained graphically and helpfully that the Czar's young daughters had *not* actually perished as a result of the gunshot wounds. Rather, they'd essentially *bled to death* because there were *so many Russian crown jewels* sewn into their corsets. These had, naturally, impeded the bullets' path, producing enormous hemorrhaging, and finally a slow, agonizing, blood-engorged death for each tiny czarina. Mother had glared at me for providing said information to my (naturally riveted) nieces.

The day before, we had been en route to the Radio City Christmas Show when we were approached by a homeless man sporting a T-shirt that said JESUS CHRIST IS COMING BACK AND BOY IS HE PISSED. He had thrust a grubby hand Mom's way and asked for a quarter. And rather than ignore him as I had instructed her to do, she had handed him one and said that while she wouldn't just *give* him a quarter, per- haps he could *earn* one by hailing us a cab. That way, she had explained, *he could hope to become a contributing member of society, such as it was with all the people of his ilk in the streets.* She had continued to lecture to him until the man actually returned her quar- ter, turned on his heel, and fled.

Back at the museum I glanced toward the revolving door and contemplated escape. But where would I go? It was pouring rain and I had no money. And I was pathologically reluctant to cause trouble. I could, I reasoned, go and sit in the entirely vulgar dark sedan my mother had insisted upon hiring, replete with a bar whose contents I had made a mental note to investigate. Not for the purpose of drink-

ing, but simply because I'd always thought people looked
unerringly cool pouring amber liquid absentmindedly out
of those leaded-crystal decanters.

Suddenly fifty feet across the museum lobby I noticed
Howard Griffith, a man I had dated years earlier. I stared at
this lanky pork-belly trader and Banana Republican, who
now stood clutching two tiny parkas that clearly belonged to
the two small, superbly blond children at his feet. *Wow,* I
thought, observing his progeny and the compact honey-
blond coed who suddenly joined them; *that coulda been me.* I
quickly turned away and hoped he hadn't seen me.

Unfortunately, Mother had caught sight of him as well.

"Isn't that the man you used to go around with from
Grosse Point? Oh, and look at his lovely brood. That could
have been you, Lambchop. But I guess you march to a different drum."

I pointed out that a career in writing and the creative arts
did not necessarily equal automatic spinsterhood, and she
looked at me understandingly and agreed.

"I suppose not," she said, then went on to remind me
that I did have that top-flight education, you know, and
that the Ivies really do take care of their own. *Why, the Cornell
Club of New York did, after all, sponsor dances where I might one day encounter a nice Yale or Princeton man.* I stared incredulously. "It's a
marvelous opportunity to meet a nice fella," she continued.
"Of course you wouldn't want to go spouting about what
you do right off the bat. Give 'em a chance to enjoy you
first, before they find out."

We slowly headed toward the blue-whale exhibit when, as

if in a dream, Mother shrieked quite loudly, whereupon
two men in leather jackets raced by us and out the revolving
door. She pointed wildly and screamed after them, but they
were gone, presumably with all of her belongings. Museum
guards surrounded us and looked stupidly at one another
before rushing out in pursuit. We all clustered around her
as she rummaged through her bag, which was, miraculously,
only torn.

Was she okay? Had they hurt her? "Don't be silly. I'm
fine," she said, brushing herself off. "They just got my wal-
let. I knew those foreigners were up to no good."

"*Mom*," Megan had intoned, *"you can't be so judgmental."*
Whereupon Mother told Meggie not to be so *uninspired*.

At that second it occurred to me what a healthy counter-
balance Dad had been for all of us. And why we owed him
an alarming debt of gratitude. In fact, it suddenly made
sense: whenever Mom became particularly difficult, his re-
course had been to head quietly to the nearest library or
bookshop. And obviously *the very threat of his disappearance to a
quiet literary place had been enough to keep her in check.*

Now every word uttered, yelped, or shrieked seemed to
echo through the museum chamber, and as I looked up I
wondered how Dad had ever endured the Thurber carnival
that we'd all become. Now both of my nieces began to cry in
unison, followed shortly by my sister. Then Eliot strolled
into the center of the museum lobby and actually *lit up a
Lucky,* which he knew was, of course, strictly prohibited, and
which, he knew, would set Mom off. It did.

All I could think of was Dad. *What would he do?*

By now, the crowd that had gathered to offer sympathy to the woman just robbed remained gathered curiously to watch this horrifying family siege. And in a sort of *kinderchain* reaction, all the random children standing near my nieces exploded into sobs.

Suddenly my attention was seized by a small sign over a doorway that read BOOKS & GIFTS. There was a plate-glass window, behind which several books were displayed. The shouting grew louder. I staggered backward, away from the combat zone. It was deafening. Then my vision began to falter, and I heard a buzzing sound in my ears. Mother turned to Eliot and asked him just who paid for his health insurance at forty-three damn years of age and maybe one of these decades or so he might consider becoming an adult. I felt hot tears begin to well up in my eyes as I awaited the assault that would surely be leveled my way next.

This would never have happened if Dad were here. I again stared at the plate-glass window underneath the sign. The crowd was closing in. The sign seemed strangely illuminated, and I could make out one of the books in the shop window. It was *The Great Big Book of Mollusks.* My family continued to shriek. The sign seemed brighter now, and I noticed another book—it was Roger Tory Peterson's *Field Guide to Birds of North America* . . . and then there was *Know Your Poisonous Snakes* . . . next to *The Predatory Cats of Southeastern Asia* and *How to Classify Mayan Ruins.* And suddenly there it was: *Canada Geese and Their Migration Patterns,* published by the National Audubon Society.

And that's what Dad would do.

At that moment I was propelled forward by an untenable and frightening force whose power I could neither fathom nor resist. Mother was calling out to me, but I was already gone, borne across the Museum floor by an otherwordly undertow. And as I headed toward the eerie light of the Museum gift and book shop I suddenly recognized this quiet welcoming chamber as a place I had always known. A place where, I knew, salvation was most definitely at hand.

fun with entropy

. . .

So maybe you *don't* know fear until you find Suzanne Pleshette standing on your doorstep with a measuring tape in her hand.

But let's say you've been living career-free for the better part of a year, and neither a financial windfall, a Pulitzer Prize, nor your own network variety program has threatened to appear and change this. And in spite of your black heart and empty life, you do have essentially cheery activities that revolve around one-acts, sketch comedy, and free red wine, thereby preventing those all-out Travis Bickle moments. In fact, this despair even has a kind of blasé quality. Because it's possible to fail madly in Southern California without the faintest hint of despair. Nor is it a situation where you biologically need need need something like black-tar heroin or the forty grand you owe a bookmaker from a Triple Crown wager gone wrong. Which is exactly why when you're at a dinner party with actors and writers and the occasional postproduction person who does God knows what but uses words like *post* without explanation, it gets really hard to drum up a sense of My Woes Blow Your Woes Out of the Water. Since everyone's nursing the identical malaise. Even a phone call to your mother, which usually produces at least the telephonic equivalent of warm milk and Shake 'n Bake, yields only bullet points of "You're the one who had to move out there" and "Risky industry, that" and finally "But do see *Bend with Beckham,* it's superb."

Then there's a month where you purposely tell everyone the absolute and often unpleasant truth. Partly because you wonder if people engage you because you have cigarettes, and partly because you've always wanted to use and mean the phrase "Let's dispense with the pleasantries now, shall we?" Before long you're telling people they're far too old to be wearing baby-doll tees, that improv is dumb, that yoga is dumberer, and that people's one-person shows—even your own—are not "poignant painful journeys of discovery," rather they are eighty-five-minute whiny me-fests. And then you actually ask each one of the cute boys working at Trader Joe's if they're all brand-new fathers, which would, of course, be the only justification for their beaming, Greenpeaceful smiles. Why you aren't instantly bludgeoned and left to bleed out in a ditch remains a mystery. Even your brother doesn't buy it, although you never did think you'd get sympathy from someone who's watched you eat six Milk-Bones in order to win a pack of Gator Gum. Plus, this behavior gets old when you realize you'd better be a little nicer or you're going to be hunting around for change from Coffee Bean & Tea Leaf in your couch and watching quirky Hungarian coming-of-age films at the Laemmle—alone—until you die. Which is why being constantly available for coffee and educated lamentation can be its own perverse spoiled lymphoma.

At which point you adopt a different tack and decide to become That Serious NPR Girl, who will speak only of Dave Eggers, Zionism, and *The Onion*—none of which you know the first thing about. Although on my first outing with my new dot.org persona I stumbled miserably, as one of my friends had just returned from doing a period film in England and suddenly I forgot all about socialized medicine because all I wanted to know was whether Kristin Scott Thomas really *was* Frosty and Chilly. So that was a bust too.

Finally, in lieu of success, or my own network variety show, I resolve to create a more genuine despair that is somehow more troubling, more afflicted, and more noteworthy than other people's. Of course the problem with having friends who are all performers is that they, like you, are so self-absorbed that it takes *that much longer* to focus and notice there's something more wrong with *you*. So between Jambas and hostile moments of reflection at Pinot, painfully considering Liberia's sudden loss of independence and Liz Phair's sudden loss of judgment, you learn just exactly how to prove your malaise is more better.

There are two kinds of malaise people can get away with. The first is a kind of personal affliction where one's despair is visibly marked by weight loss and pallor. Since the only eating disorder I've ever experienced is the inability to stop doing it, and my pink skin gives me all the complexity and mystique of a yellow Labrador, this is not really an option. The second kind of malaise happens when somebody just plain has a deeper sensitivity to world events. My psychotherapist, with whom I now speak via the phone, and who has now morphed into the tainted love child of Albert Brooks and Lesley Stahl, caught me here in my attempt to cop this manifestation. Because I said that I was quite sad—really inexorably sad—and I was sure it was one of those existential angsty things, and she said, "No it's not. You're not any more deeply affected by terrorism or the Abu Ghraib situation than anyone else. If you were working in a soup kitchen in Chicago, if you were a social worker in Sacramento, then it's possible you would be exhibiting a three-dimensional feeling. But you aren't. So you can't. Nor is this some kind of posttraumatic-stress response to 9/11 you've drummed up. You're just worried about rent and the fact that someone you once met got a guest spot on *Charmed*."

She was right, natch.

So I'm thinking wouldn't it be fun if I had something like an income or a soul, and I'm watching my dog, the small feral Jack Russell terrier whom I'm always with in Runyon Canyon, where nice people always say *which one is yours* and I must invariably respond that he's the one *busily fellating theirs*. Yet here's an animal with a brain the size of a Smokehouse Almond whose life is completely turned around by a single tennis ball. And I realize maybe I just need my own kind of tennis ball.

Which is when I begin to tutor children in Beverly Hills.

When I start tutoring I am not so naïve as to think that I'll be doing any kind of Dead Poets song and dance, but I am under the erroneous impression that my work will be at least valuable and at best groundbreaking. What with molding these sleek young bored minds and all. I learn that when dealing with privately schooled seventeen-year-olds, boys are easier to tutor than girls, because they have a better capacity to focus. And since I really can't focus when there are shiny things in a room or, in these situations, genuine Vermeers and Warhols, it's easier to work with boys.

I also have the odd notion that I'll be treated like royalty, psychologically fed and clothed like some kind of medieval alchemist with all of life's secrets in her grubby east-of-Doheny hand. I arrive daily at fabulous homes, greeted by maids who look down their noses because they spray and dust items far more valuable than me. They usher me around once they make sure I have taken my dirty teacher shoes off. I am usually given water, which is replenished regularly in an effort to keep me functioning inside my workplace. Kind of like someone in a cult who is given just enough green beans to stay alive but not enough to rebel.

But I know it really *is* about the kids. So that when one mother, the panicked and rail-thin wife of a monolithic producer, explains that this is a serious business, and that *Goddamnit school is vital* and *this is costing thousands of dollars* and *there isn't time to screw around,* I am delighted by her commitment. Until she explains that for this very reason it would be a lot simpler and much cheaper if I just went ahead and wrote her children's papers myself. And after the ninety seconds it takes me to determine just what ethics are and whether I have any—the answer being no—I quickly set about writing term papers. This provides some comfort, until you wind up at a party again and somebody says they just sold a script to Miramax, and you say you just got an A on your Rasputin paper but you only got a B+ on your Dylan Thomas paper because it got handed in late, which is when you also realize you're just steps away from forty, calcium tablets, and all the status of a kiddie pool in Van Nuys.

Still, within a matter of months I begin to undergo a curious sea change. For the first time, I settle down, get calm, and gain just a teensy bit of perspective. And slowly but surely I begin to feel needed. Maybe there is salvation somewhere between Interstates 101 and 405. After all, I am now working and decent and waged and I have a sensible German car and a dog and a nifty little pad in West Hollywood and maybe it is okay. I am even beginning to hunch and shuffle less, and soon I begin to decorate my emotional corner of the world with the patterned chintz of pride. Most important, I am becoming part of these families. So I encourage sixteen-year-old boys to tell me why they opted for the A4 instead of the C class while I churn out provocative, insightful essays. And suddenly, I am doing very well in school. And I think the eleventh grade should not be tackled until after thirty. It's a pretty heady thing, academic achievement. It all feels very familial until the day one mother discovers I tutored *other* children in her son's class. This would, I believe, please her, but instead, so deep is her paranoia that she looks at me with startled horror (as

though I have demanded to perform her next dermabra-
sion). And that afternoon, when her son's entire film class
shows up to shoot a feature-length film at their house, she
becomes alarmed and I am politely asked not to show my
face around any of the kids. Then, when it comes time to
leave, two maids brusquely usher me through a series of for-
bidden corridors and secret libraries, out to the kitchen,
where I am placed in a waiting sedan and swiftly driven
around the entire block back to my own car—kind of like
the president, or Madonna.

And I'm driving home, kind of startled by this but at the
same time gripped by a sense of practicality and achievement. And for the first time in my life I realize, *Hey, this is
business.* This is how they do things. *You're* the one who wanted
to freelance. You've got your life, your dog, and your
home. You've got enough self-adhesive stamps to last you
through the next Olympics. And maybe it's not so bad, and
why were you so stupid and arrogant as to spend months
imagining that anyone *but* your dog *should* really revolve
around you—with all these ridiculous personas?

Instantly betterness appears. Because I have weathered an
affront and *pffft.* I am fine. I quit whining. And I become
so deliriously happy about the simple things in life that I
stop at one of those little faux-Moroccan boutiques on
Third Street with the infantile salesgirls you know who are
dumber and cooler than you'll ever be, and I buy myself a
little floral/wistful candle so everyone entering my apartment will remember that they're really just whiling away the
afternoon in an eighteenth-century garden in the Cotswolds.

Which is when I return home to find (1) Suzanne Pleshette, (2) a former consigliere from a major motion picture studio, and (3) an architect, waiting at my front door. With measuring tape. These are the people in my neighborhood, specifically, upstairs—the people on my condo board—from whom I rent. They ask if they can inspect my apartment, which I know they think I'm living inside like some filthy little Dostoyevsky figure who smokes way too much. Bewildered but cheery, I usher them in, and, curiously, they begin to discuss whether walls could actually be knocked out, surfaces refinished, and other improvements made. They smile at me. I pause, and then I get it. At which point the carbon chip that is my heart swells to 2.5 times its normal size—once I realize that all this talk is to make *my* situation better. Astonishingly, these people are going to improve my very own home. I am stunned, feeling both flushy and blushy. Finally, after four years, I have become an accepted member of the building, who will soon enjoy the luxuries of the other apartments. Suzanne and the others pleasantly poke around, thank me, and leave. And I know it is all coming together. I am going to have a new home to complement my new life. And here I've always been irritated that my agents work above Calico Corner; why, now I'll be into that mighty fabric kingdom like a shot—picking out brand-new material for curtains for which my condo board will happily pay!

The following day I am issued a certified document that gives me thirty days to vacate the premises, on account of how the board is planning to convert my apartment into a juice bar and spa for the building. Suddenly, all of my thoughts, my whining, whining thoughts about where my life is headed, go out the window. And I realize—like you do—that whenever you're feeling down but still holier than thou, you should also remember that you have—or had—a really nice little pad in West Hollywood. And that maybe smuggie smuggersons need to pay a little attention to what really is important. And then again, maybe the cute smiling boys working at Trader Joe's know something I don't.

april fool

. . .

Suburban Philadelphia has a kind of half-baked snow during the holidays, to accompany its "neither" personality as far as states go. For it is neither North, where it could boast a frosty New England flintiness, nor South, with stoic colonial architecture and locals who talk about kin and a now-reconstructed past. No, Philadelphia is strictly the jewel of the middle states' crown (or so its residents think), and it sits there, not as dull as Baltimore, not as cloistered as Wilmington, not as starchy and important as D.C., and never, ever, ever as cool as New York.

Three weeks after my fourteenth birthday I returned home for a break from my first semester at boarding school to enter the house, drop my suitcase, and watch George Margrove, one of Philadelphia's most prominent attorneys, pitch headfirst off our living room coffee table. My mother and father were having a dinner party, and everyone was dressed up to celebrate the evening before some time-honored football matchup the following afternoon. I remember that Mr. Margrove had gotten up, laughed lustily, and gone to replace the drink that had, by now, been almost fully absorbed by the white shag carpet of our living room. He'd swerved to avoid me and patted me on the scalp before saying, "Hiya kid, how's prep school? How's that wandering eye?" on his way to the bar. I remember that event vividly, and the resumed merriment was interrupted only by the scream of Mrs. Henry Moncrieff, an adulterous pickax of a socialite. Apparently, despite my brother's claim that our four dogs were "curled up, watching TV in the den," they had also managed to shred her sable into a million tiny pieces, presumably during a commercial.

And while my mother was typically loath to use bad language in front of the children (the exception being the word *Goddamn*, which in suburban Philadelphia lexicon seemed merely a descriptive adjective along the lines of *sunny* or *striped*), she would frequently point out that Mr. Margrove really and truly defined the word *jackass*. I asked her if he was an alcoholic, and she turned to me and explained that *here and now*, in relative terms, *no*.

"And how come you guys have him to your parties?"

"Because he has us to his. It's all a big ecosystem, Lambchop, and your father winds up with a lot of patients that way. All psychiatrists do. *Which is why you're in private school.*"

Of course the Margroves were pillars of society. Mrs. Margrove was a striking Austrian woman with Olympic skiing credentials and a delicious *come-hither (and-let's-get-out-of-here)* accent whose entire life, it seemed, was devoted

exclusively to propagating the species. And to nurturing
others like her, who were busy with the lifetime plan of producing children devoid of blemishes, weakness, character,
or remorse. Mr. Margrove had made an enormous fortune,
first by marrying Mrs. Margrove, and then through shrewd
speculation, profiting handsomely on the wheat embargo
that starved most of North Vietnam. They had five children. Mom said each one was as mirthless, as colorless, and
as odorless as could be.

Mr. Margrove suffered fools viciously. He was tremen-
dously arrogant and a bully, and the story was often told
about how he had arrived home, quite drunk, with Mrs.
Margrove very late one Saturday night. He had insisted
upon driving the family babysitter (whose name was Magda)
home, despite the fact that he had lost all neurological impulses *and* his necktie in the course of one long evening.
Magda was known for her patience, her naïveté about drunk
Americans, and her alleged habit of lifting employers' jewelry and selling it on the Ukrainian black market in downtown Philadelphia. In fact, the story went that she would
have succeeded all along had she not been so engorged with
hubris as to brazenly sport a stolen Cartier amulet upon her
wrist for all the world (and her employers) to see. But that's
beside the point.

So Mr. Margrove had been hell-bent on driving Magda
home. They had climbed into the car, and he'd spent five
violent minutes trying to locate his keys. Then he'd repeatedly tried to jam the key into the ignition to start the car.
Then came a series of expletives and an utterance that in-

cluded the words "Jesus Christmas," "Goddamn whore of a car," and "son of a bitch all's I wanna do is get our fucking frau back to her Goddamn fucking home." This had continued until Magda finally took advantage of one momentary pause in rhetoric to point out that one reason Mr. Margrove was probably having these ignition difficulties was because he was sitting in *the backseat.*

Mr. Margrove was also an unbelievable snob, and Harry Graves, our travel agent, told us that once, when he was booking a flight for the Margroves to the British West Indies, he'd had to call Mr. Margrove with a little query. Which turned out to be the names on the Margroves' airplane tickets. Because there was the Mr. and the Mrs. and their five kids, as well as two other individuals, known only as "Cook" and "Nanny." Our travel agent had regrettably explained to Mr. Margrove that British Airways, despite its own colonialistic tendencies, was not permitted to issue tickets in the name of "Cook" and "Nanny." Evidently this caused quite a stir, for not only was Mr. Margrove infuriated by this interruption of his day's schedule, he was also at a complete loss as to what Cook and Nanny's names actually *were.*

One year we learned that the five Margrove children had euphorically brought home a basket of puppies from a bake sale on a Saturday afternoon. Mrs. Margrove, whose real name was Ophelia but who everyone called Bitty, had been delighted with the six tiny creatures, and Mr. Margrove had barely taken notice of them. However, the following morning when Mrs. Margrove was loading everybody up for church, Mr. Margrove had demurred, which everybody thought extremely odd. It turned out that during the time his wife and children were away at church, Mr. Margrove had taken the basket of puppies and driven to the nearest Catholic church—which was, naturally, miles away—gone into the parking lot, and placed a puppy inside each one of the fanciest cars he could find, thus assuring each puppy affluent, if not entirely prepared, homes.

Mother had told me once that the real problem with Mr. Margrove—the real thorn in his bourbon-tremored paw—was the fact that his only son was gay. I'd wondered why that was such a problem, as at that point in school the only person anybody knew who even might be gay was David Bowie, and he was about as cool as it got, as far as the ninth grade was concerned. Not that I thought George Margrove would have been a particularly understanding parent to David Bowie. And despite the fact that this was by now the late seventies, we lived in a horrifying community seemingly impervious to trend or liberal thought. Things were quite different then. Nobody used clickers, people who cooked used only one kind of mushroom and that was a mushroom, the only color barriers being broken down were those of Levi's corduroys, *balsamic* referred adjectivally to a kind of tree, and your film was always ruined in the airport. Spiro Agnew was viewed with some ambivalence. Madonna was busy shotgunning communion wine somewhere in Michigan. The Ice Capades were taking the nation by storm. And Reuben Kinkaid embodied the sensitive male.

I'd wondered about Mr. Margrove's gay son. Tony was

awkward and five years older than me, so I wasn't exactly on his radar, although he'd always remembered my name, which was more than sufficient praise. I think he was also nice to me because he was blind in one eye (as a result of some kind of childhood mishap on a Wyoming dude ranch). And thus perhaps he felt sorry for me, since my own ocular condition allowed me to stare at two people on either side of a room simultaneously. In fact, when we ran into each other every Easter at the golf club, he was always kind and gentle toward me in that way that certain animals can be with other animals who are young or injured. We heard horrible rumors about public humiliations, and how the father had once drunkenly disinherited Tony until such time as *the little wimp learns how to do the right thing by his family.*

Nobody knew why Mr. Margrove had been so intractable with his own flesh and blood. Mother said it was because the son undermined his father's masculinity. I'd reminded Mother that there was another man in our town who she had said was gay, Mr. Fitzhugh. And I wondered how he could be gay if he was married and the father of four. Mother had explained that he'd married because, for men of that era, that was the thing to do, even though one might march to a different drum. Kind of like Tony Randall, she'd said.

Mr. Margrove bullied his son mercilessly, and whenever I ran into Tony he was being forced to participate in some kind of activity that reeked of intrepid virility, be it fly-fishing or running with bulls or ice hockey. I think Mr. Margrove probably would've taken his son to wager on cockfighting or bear baiting if these were still sanctioned activities. I knew Tony was a bright and curious kid, but he walked in a stooped and tentative way that people do who are always worried that a door is going to fly open violently in front of them. He didn't speak a lot, and his sentences were always *considered*. He was fair and, like me, shouldn't have spent a lot of time outside, as each of us was one big freckle of cancer. We were vaguely friendly over the years, although I also felt that Tony—even ostracized, forbidden-fruit-chasing Tony—thought I was *common* and therefore not entirely worth his attention. We'd heard that he'd been forced to go to Dartmouth, where, Mother said, he'd be doomed to rot with the ivy and the J. P. Morgans until he came into his own or escaped. That was the last anyone had heard of Tony. A week after graduation he'd disappeared.

Then a few months ago, on the morning of April Fool's Day, I ran into Tony Margrove on Fifty-ninth Street in New York. He looked nothing like the awkward teen I'd seen last. He radiated health and genuine goodwill, had grown considerably, and was achingly handsome. He shook my hand in that see-I've-made-it way that always makes me uncomfortable because I've never achieved much of anything, to date. He was now a film producer, he explained, living in California, had a lover of ten years, and was in town doing research for a new documentary film about Alzheimer's disease. At that instant I tried to say, "How fascinating" and mean it, because I really did, but it occurred to me that "how fascinating" was probably about all that documentary filmmakers ever hear from the ignorant populace. He explained that the money from the big companies, largely pharmaceutical manufacturers, was there for the taking if you happened to be interested in something that they were interested in. And it was clear he had taken them up on their offers.

"So," he explained, "I have an enormous budget, thanks to Pfizer and Eli Lilly, so I really can do pretty much whatever I want, and Alzheimer's is really where everything converges these days—researchwise. It's really an extraordinary opportunity to *give back,* you know?"

We walked along for a few blocks together, and I explained that my career was all but inert, but in a good way, I assured him, and that I was glad to be out of Philadelphia. He stopped and looked at me as though I'd experienced some kind of tingling loss, before saying that he was so sorry to hear that. He told me he thought *home* and *family* were important, and that he could never imagine giving up that base.

"I'll always go back there—that's what I'm about," he said, smiling.

I was shocked and wondered about the pod person who was now standing before me singing the praises of the gutless and acrid community from which we'd sprung. I did not mention the heinous and cruel man who had tried to drive his own child into the chute of acceptance. We said our good-byes, and I marveled at his happy state, noting how decidedly unfettered and unwounded he'd turned out, despite his horrific early years. Although I did wonder about his creepily cheery penchant for suburban Philadelphia.

The following morning Mother appeared in New York for one of her quarterly theater junkets. I had agreed to join her for lunch before she darted off to yet another singing, dancing, kickline-celebrating matinee. We went to a crowded bistro, where I was sure that she would see enough interesting people in horrifying clothing to keep her entertained throughout the meal, like a mobile in a crib does for a baby. The conversation turned to our old hometown, which she was actually contemplating leaving now that my father had passed away, due to the fact that she was "not old enough to be a matriarch, not young enough to be a trophy wife, and not mean enough to be a Philadelphia widow." I mentioned having seen Mr. Margrove's son, Tony, and she said that whole thing must really have been a tragedy. I explained that it was not a tragedy at all, that he'd been lovely and was now clearly thriving. Mother then sighed and said, "No, no. The tragedy is the *father*, not the son."

"Whaddya mean, Mom?"

"Not the *son*, Lambchop. It's Tony's father—didn't I tell you he had horrible Alzheimer's? It's terrible, really. The family has been shattered. Just destroyed."

I stared at her in shock and wondered if I'd gotten away from it all in time, or if I too, like Tony Margrove, would grow old with that Philadelphian tendency to fail, forget, and be cheery about it all still.

"All right then, dearie. I'm off. You sure you don't want to come with? I can probably get you a ticket at the box office. It's not too late."

"No thanks, Mom. You go on. Have fun at the show."

And I knew she would. She was off again to see *42nd Street*, the musical. And I knew, and she knew, and American Express knew, that this was the sixth time in two years she'd gone to see it. But I'd never tell.

I began to walk home through Rockefeller Center, past its majestic fountains, its gilded statues, and its center-of-the-world architecture. I watched men selling falafel and hot dogs to hungry wide-eyed tourists and harassed bankers. I outpaced taxis and buses up Sixth Avenue, keeping my eyes on the tips of the trees that garnished Fifty-ninth Street and the mouth of Central Park. I stared straight ahead into a blur of neckties and silk blouses and hooded sweatshirts. Until my eyes alighted upon Clark R. M. Wheeler, M.D., standing on a curb, waiting for the light to change. My heart sped up and then began to beat in a weird double-time pattern as I watched him from forty feet, hands deep in his pockets as he stared down at his tassel loafers. He was wearing a pink button-down with the neck open. *Well, hello! What a nice surprise! And how are you? Connecticut? That's awesome. You did? You got one? Oh, I love a Lab puppy. She is? Four months now? Congratulations!*

He looked up from his shoes and turned his head, peering east across the avenue. *I quit. Yes, I did, Clark. You bet. Never felt better. Lots of freelance. Traveling a lot. Who knows? Maybe I'll start my own business.*

The light finally changed, and Clark stepped out onto the street and began to approach. He was about twenty feet in front of me, and for a split second I had this vision of one riotous morning when we had squabbled for an hour over which deluxe-optioned coffeemaker to buy before getting one home and being unable to even turn it on. And as the image dimmed in my mind I put my head down and swiftly walked around and outside the herd that was crossing the street, never turning around, and soon I was speeding up the avenue toward the tree-tipped park.

acknowledgments

• • •

For their wisdom, encouragement, and unilateral support, this author would like to thank Sarah Allan, Courtney Watkins and Jeff Robinson, Lee Graham, Fred Nelson, Frances Jones, Alice King, Craig Carlisle, Henry Luce III, Mark Carnessale, Jessalyn Gilsig, Sally Brooks, Liz Kerrigan, Lisa McKean, Lindsay Denman, Maria Semple, Thomas McCormack, Jessie McCormack, Bob Myman, Mary Ann Naples, Adam Korn, Christopher Piehler, Shelley Barth, Mike Goldstein, the marvelous people at Time Inc., and Michael Kors.

I have performed many of these monologues theatrically; for their generosity and production wherewithal I am most grateful to Naked Angels, Tim Ransom, Annabelle Gurwitch, Michele Remsen, Margaret Mendelson, John Ruocco, John Martin, Gary Mann, Sit n' Spin, Uncabaret, and Indie 103.1 FM. Copious thanks to my siblings—Jeffrey, Leslie, Michael, Carol, Nina, and Blair—for their remarkable insight, patience, and tolerance.

Plus huge thanks to my ultracharismatic editor, Bruce Tracy, for putting me in participating bookstores.

about the author

• • •

Writer and actress ELIZABETH WARNER spent nine years on staff as a promotional copywriter for Time Inc.'s magazine group in New York. In 2002 she premiered her one-woman show, *The Wandering Eye*, at HBO's Aspen Comedy Festival. She continues to perform regularly in both New York and Los Angeles, has appeared on NPR, wrote for several network TV game shows, and sold a children's program to Disney. In L.A. she is the voice of morning news on Indie 103.1 FM radio, and keen viewers can spot her in a few films. A Cornell graduate, she lives in Los Angeles but, no fool, maintains a New York residence as well.